Helping the Small Church
Win Guests

Helping the Small Church Win Guests

Preparing to Increase Attendance

DESMOND BARRETT

foreword by Tom Cheyney

WIPF & STOCK · Eugene, Oregon

HELPING THE SMALL CHURCH WIN GUESTS
Preparing to Increase Attendance

Copyright © 2024 Desmond Barrett. All rights reserved. Except for brief quotations in critical publications or reviews, no part of this book may be reproduced in any manner without prior written permission from the publisher. Write: Permissions, Wipf and Stock Publishers, 199 W. 8th Ave., Suite 3, Eugene, OR 97401.

Wipf & Stock
An Imprint of Wipf and Stock Publishers
199 W. 8th Ave., Suite 3
Eugene, OR 97401

www.wipfandstock.com

PAPERBACK ISBN: 979-8-3852-1208-8
HARDCOVER ISBN: 979-8-3852-1209-5
EBOOK ISBN: 979-8-3852-1210-1

04/15/24

Small church pastors tend to feel unseen and underappreciated. Know that you are seen and valued by God and me. I have walked in your shoes, and I have experienced what you have faced, but know this truth: keep doing your best, prepare for the future, and understand God is honoring your call.

Remember, pastor, you are doing better than you realize.

—D. B.

Contents

Foreword by Tom Cheyney | ix

Chapter 1
Post-Pandemic Church: The Changing Church | 1

Chapter 2
Preparing the Way: Getting Ready for Guests | 14

Chapter 3
Welcome Home: Reimagining the Space | 28

Chapter 4
Be the One: Investing in Relationships | 43

Chapter 5
Discipleship: Developing Christlike Followers
to Reach Outside | 53

Chapter 6
The Community in Crises: Be Jesus in the Face of Trouble | 63

Chapter 7
Close the Back Door: Keeping Guests You Have Won | 73

Chapter 8
Developing Guests into Future Leaders | 83

Chapter 9
Leading with Passion So Others Follow | 90

Epilogue | 101

About the Author | 105

Other Books by the Author | 106

Foreword

READ THIS BOOK WITH a pen or highlighter since you will need to go back and grab the gems that abound throughout this book. Dr. Desmond Barrett, who is quickly becoming the leading voice on church revitalization and renewal within the Church of the Nazarene movement, has done it again. What a great book for the local church getting serious about reaching guests that come to their church! Consider, if you will, that churches spend huge sums of money planning and then building facilities and parking lots so that guests will feel welcomed in their place of worship. Yet far too many leadership teams forget the impact that is gained in focusing and formulating a plan for a guest-friendly church. I hear all the time from church leaders who say they are a friendly church. But in reality, most prospects and visitors are not looking for a friendly church, they are looking for a church where they can develop real lasting friends while being drawn closer to the Lord Jesus. Far too many churches treat their guests as a means to achieve their own goals, forgetting about the needs of the visitors. Such action implies that guests are expected to meet the needs of the church, not that the church is there to meet the needs of the guests.

Pastors must begin thinking like a visitor. Desmond Barrett is a pastor who thinks about how the guest coming to a church would feel. In *Helping the Small Church Win Guests: Preparing to Increase Attendance*, Barrett has written a great work for the local church which holds the visiting guest as the most important person in

Foreword

church every Sunday. His desire is to make guests feel welcomed, not embarrassed. He longs for them to feel comfortable and not out of place. He knows that the guest needs to feel included rather than singled out. This book is full of Barrett's passion for equipping churches in how to discover the most effective ways for reaching the visiting prospect.

My experience has been to utilize one's facilities to tell the great story of Jesus and then to follow that up by using them to tell your story through graphics that display your core values and why they are the most important parts of your vision for your community. I want my church and you want your church to be a church with an open door so all who need Jesus, want Jesus, and will follow Jesus can have a place to worship that they will call home. Open your door so everyone wants to come in and then stay in, never seeking to go back out. Connection is a vital part of growing churches. Within these nine chapters you will find the thoughts, tools, and teachings that you can convey to your own church as you prepare to increase attendance.

Dr. Tom Cheyney, Founder & Directional Leader
Renovate National Church Revitalization Conferences
The Renovate Group

Chapter 1

Post-Pandemic Church
The Changing Church

THE SANCTUARY WAS DARK for the most part, except for the stage lights that were on as the worship team practiced for the upcoming service in just a few hours. I was not expecting any guests or anyone really to show up beyond the volunteers that needed to be in attendance. It was the first week of a three-week church closure that coincided with the recommendation of the denomination to close local churches due to the increasing cases of COVID-19 in our region. As the doors to the sanctuary opened, light streamed from the lobby; into the darkened sanctuary stepped an impressive man of stature carrying his Bible in his hand.

Three things struck me that morning as I viewed him from the front row. One, he was a stranger, as I did not recognize this guest entering the building. The second was this guest could have sat on the last row of the 400-seat sanctuary, or even in the middle section, as fewer than fifteen people were in the space. Instead, he walked up the long center isle and chose the second row, sitting in the second seat. The last thing that struck me was that he had a physical copy of the Bible in his hand. For many churches this is a common sight, but for my church it was not. I, being one of a handful, still carried a hardback copy of the Bible. Smartphones with search features and downloaded Bible apps have turned churchgoers away from the paper form to pressing the digital button. As soon as the stranger in our midst sat down, I walked over to him with a large cheeky smile and warmly greeted him while apologizing that the service was closed to in-person worship. If he wanted to stay and worship with us, he could, but we were going live digitally over the next three weeks.

The guest, who called himself John, spoke in short sentences that I struggled to put together between the mask and the ongoing music practice. I smiled at him through my eyes and sat back down. As I finished preaching that day, the Lord impressed on my heart to be open to this guest and what he had to say, but as I looked up, he had slipped out. In speaking with my wife, I wondered if the contemporary worship music or our casual style of dress chased him off. Yet, the following week, here came John through the doors, comfortable and casual as if he had been in the building a thousand times. With his Bible in hand, he made his way to the second row, second chair, and sat down. This time I was determined to get more out of this stranger, but like the Sunday before the conversation was short and direct. Except now he wanted to know why I had not done an altar call the week before. Choosing my words carefully, I began to speak of the difficulty of doing an altar call when there was no one there, as I was speaking to a camera and small group of fewer than fifteen people in person.

John just looked at me, moved his head ever so slightly and then turned and walked away. This time I said to my wife on the ride home, "What is wrong with this man? He asked a question; I gave him an answer and I got no response except a slight head move and then he turned away." Week three came and this time I was prepared for John. I would not wait for him to enter the sanctuary. Instead he would be greeted in the lobby, and I would be ready for his question-and-answer time. John came through the lobby doors, I said hello, he shook my hand, and off he went. Nothing. That was it. Not a word. Not a question, just a handshake and into the sanctuary he walked. In all honesty, I was speechless, and believe me, I'm not often one to have trouble finding something to say. After the service, I walked down the steps of the platform and John came up again with his favorite question: "No altar call today? Do you not do them?" he said. Flustered, looking for words, I tried to explain, but again there was no reaction, no response, except this time he looked up to the heavens and off he went exited the building.

Week four came, and honestly, I was dreading the meeting with my strange visitor. This time we were back to in-person services, and I wrote myself a note to do an altar call after the message. In fact, there would be two altar calls in the next three weeks to make up for any suggestion from my guests that I was unspiritual. At the end of the sermon, an altar call was conducted, and where was John? He did not move. The man who wanted an altar call did not move to the altar. The next week the same thing happened, but this time it appeared John had fallen asleep. At this point I wanted to yell into the microphone, "Mr. John, this is your time! The requested altar call has now taken place. Please move forward to the front in an orderly manner." But he never moved, not once.

The following week, I did not feel the nudge or the Holy Spirit compelling me to do an altar call. Rather predictably, John came up to me with his favorite question, "Do you not do altar calls?" said the man who never moved forward during the last two. Instead of being disrespectful, I smiled and said, "John, when God moves, I move." John then asked, "Where did you get your education?" As I began laying out each degree and college/university I graduated from, he looked disinterested in what was being said. When I paused, he turned and walked away. Not another word about education, or even altar calls.

A few weeks later, John did not come back to church. Worried about what had happened to him, I found his social media page and found out he had contracted COVID-19. Within the week he would pass away. In his last social media post, John wrote, "Just before midnight, I felt a sensation that everything was turning around." For my friend, and pandemic guest, things did turn around. He was healed. I can picture on the movie screen of my imagination John pestering Jesus with questions much like he did me, and all I can do is smile.

It has now been two years since I stood before his open casket and shared a message of hope with his family and friends in a holler in eastern Kentucky. The legacy that John left behind is numerous, but to this established church pastor he reminded me that serving the kingdom is not about titles, degrees, or how many people attend a service. It is about listening, learning, and leaning into what other people share. It is the challenge to be nimble amid crises as you seek to see Jesus even in a simple conversation. The challenge is to always stay open to seeing Jesus in strangers that come across your path.

THE WORLD STOPPED

In February of 2020 it became clear that something was happening. It seemed every news station was sending out alarm bells that a once-in-a-lifetime pandemic was upon us. Sure, whispers of a pandemic were building throughout the month of January, but by mid-February the country was going into lockdown. The Global Christian Church has weathered many storms across the centuries, so my leadership team was not worried; as our thinking was, this too shall pass. That was until an all-points bulletin went out from coast-to-coast and state-to-state that the world seemed to be shutting down. The one question I heard over and over was, "What are we going to do?" If I were honest, I did not know, but as a leader I needed to develop a game plan. Meeting with my church leadership team, and consulting with my denominational leader, it was clear there was no easy answer. I began to look back in history when the last pandemic had hit the world, the Spanish flu (influenza pandemic) of 1918–19. Reading everything I could on the subject, I realized this new pandemic was going to cripple the world, much less the local church. Could we survive a long-term closure? Could the church be the church without a building?

Those and many other questions were raised from across the lips of the leadership team.

Now take out the word "pandemic" and add your church's issue, and you will quickly see that you can either allow the problem to cripple the church or use it as an opportunity to reexamine the way church has always been done. Believe me, it will not be easy! But it will be worth the steps taken out in this resource if you and the leadership team you lead are willing to navigate the season of change your church has entered.

NAVIGATING A CHANGE SEASON INSIDE THE CHURCH

As a leader, you want to see God's will done in the local church. Most churches sincerely desire God's will be done, but far too many are not willing to get out of the way and allow God to move. Change, however, takes work. Any amount of change causes pain, pushback, and potential land mines that could implode your change direction. But even if people dislike change, a leader should still lead change. For every season in the church's life, pandemic or not, God brings forth the right leader and ideas to help the church flourish. You may have asked yourself, *Where do I start?* The simple answer is anywhere you desire God is leading. The reality is that somebody or something will push back against the change wherever you begin. You can either be discouraged or encouraged to see change affect people, good or bad, in the church's life. Each situation provides feedback on how you communicate in the community about the change.

Change Awaits the One Seeking Change

Around every corner of the church, there are opportunities to help move the local congregation forward into a season of blessing. One might ask: what is the plan? Too often, leaders (pastors, church boards, or church influencers) make decisions based on their feelings, not where God wants them to lead his people. A leader can share ideas and listen for feedback with a clear strategy developed strategically through personal conversations, smaller group gatherings, and more significant informational times.

Be strategic in taking the time to lean into new conversations that are vitally important in the local church's life. What you do today has lasting effects tomorrow. So, wade into conversations that can help shape your thinking and that of the church.

Take Steps to Ease into Change

Change does not happen overnight, but change happens every night. Confusing? Well, it should not be. Everybody wants change, yet change is only for some. Each day things change even if we do not want them to. Change happens because of the passage of time. Time does not stand still for anyone, including your ideas to help the church adapt to where they find themselves today. Think about it this way; there are twelve months in a year and fifty-two weeks in a year. Three hundred sixty-five days make up those weeks. To accomplish change and to reach a goal, the church must see each year, month, week, day, and hour as stepping one step closer to the promise or a postponement. The fastest way to help change the church is to take the first step toward change.

How many times have you or the church missed its blessing? How often have you heard an issue talked to death instead of acting? Well, the leadership took action by burying it with the sounds of each other's voices and the actual moving of the idea into fruition. Let me challenge you to be bold in leading the people to God's promise before the church. With each step the leadership team takes to accomplish God's goal placed before the church, you are stepping closer to God's destiny that is before you.

Dreams Take action and Action Starts with Change

Looking back over the past year, where do you see that the church has missed God? If you can honestly answer and then evaluate what went wrong, you will be able to figure out how not to do it again. It sounds simple, but it is hard because it takes a self-reflection autopsy of your leadership skills, and most leaders do not want to go through the pain to receive the gain. Daily, God is speaking to a leader like you. He is unfolding his plan for your life and that of your ministry. The dreams he planted inside you are being called forth to germinate and take root. Do not hesitate to allow God to water your dreams.

Dream stealers are running rampant in the world today. They will tell you, "You are not good enough. You are not gifted. You will just fail, so quit before you start." Do not allow the negative to overwhelm the joyous calling God has affirmed over your life. Like prophets before, God has anointed you for this season in the life of your church. Pray, read, listen, and seek God daily. Find time to reflect on what is being said in the church and your spirit. Enable God's promise to take hold to bring your dreams to reality. In a world that can be so discouraging, be encouraged that your God dreams will come to pass.

Leader, God is getting ready to pour out his blessing like never before upon the church, so do not be discouraged. As you reflect over the last week, month, and maybe even a year, remember, be prepared (by doing your part) to help navigate the changing season in the life of your church. Be willing to take action steps and to keep dreaming dreams for your local church as you lead them through a change season.

FAMILIARITY IS HURTING THE CHURCH WHEN GUESTS ARRIVE

When first-time guests walk into the local church, they see the church with a fresh perspective. They view the worn carpet, the smell of an unaired basement, the cluttered classroom, and the bathroom that seems more at home in the 1960s than in the current age. Many churchgoers have become comfortable in familiar surroundings and miss the opportunity to invest in the infrastructure of the local church. But guests do not. They see, hear, and smell, all when visiting a church for the first time. There is a saying, "first impressions are lasting ones." What the church facilities look like is as vital as how the church greets guests when they enter the church.

Ask yourself, has my church become so comfortable in the familiar that we miss what guests are experiencing when they visit for the first time? Guests will break through the confines of the comfortable and see Christ, or they will see the church stuck in the familiar and never return. So, how does a church know familiarity hurts the church when guests arrive?

Familiarity in Loss

Since the onset of the pandemic-induced inflation, following two years of a global pandemic, the church has faced two strong headwinds that have sped up membership decline. Established churches, those that have been around for decades, have most likely seen their numbers fluctuate over time. The death of members, health issues related to members, moving away to be with family or a care home, loss of income, and thus lack of workers would have been absorbed and unnoticed in decades past. But with the perfect storm of all of these coming at the same time on top of two worldwide events, the established church has been rocked by loss after loss, leaving her, in many cases, a shell of who she was beforehand.

The familiarity with loss is exacerbated by long-term members not coming back to church regularly and the lack of families with young children attending. As guests enter the church for the first time, they can sense that the church is lacking through social interactions and observation. While they might not be able to put their finger on what is lacking, they can see the stress and strains of the loss. Instead of focusing on the loss, the church leadership should focus on what could come from new families visiting the church. The church must embrace its season, not make excuses for the failures, but begin to define a new normal to move forward instead of staying in the past. God is not surprised by what is happening in the local church; instead, he has given the tools to the local church in the form of people, programs, and positions to propel the church forward in this new season.

Familiarity in Uncertainty

When loss comes to the church, a time of personal and spiritual reflection takes place. It is natural to talk, observe, and pray through the loss. However, many established churches have found themselves stuck in uncertainty, and it has become their friend instead of an action step to behold. Nowhere in Scripture can I find that God wants the church to sit in uncertainty for an extended period. Instead, I read that he constantly propelled his people forward to capture new ground for the kingdom. As guests enter a church for the first time, they are already uncertain about what to find. If the church leaders are making excuses for why something is not done or done a certain way, how does that build confidence in your first-time guests? It does not. It makes them more certain not to return.

There is no better time than today to begin to capture God's new vision for the local church. If you have a lot of empty classroom space in your building, reimagine the area. See what the neighborhood around the church needs and if your local church can help meet those needs by providing space for an afterschool program, counseling space for addiction recovery, or grief- share programs. Outside the church's campus is a world that needs your local church. Be a church that reflects the community's needs by opening herself up to meet those needs in partnership with the neighborhood. Do not get stuck in the uncertainty of time but be confident that God still has more for your local church to accomplish.

Familiarity with the Familiar

I have heard it said that people should come to church for Jesus, not for what the church looks like on the inside. While I will not disagree with the heart behind the comment, people look at the facility's façade and judge the church's effectiveness from that point of view. Right or wrong, it happens weekly. So, if you know that church shopping and consumerism Christianity takes place, what will the local church do about it? Sit back and wait, or take preemptive care in caring for the facility? The answer should be caring for the facility as an extension of honoring God's plans for the established church.

Spend some time walking the facility with crucial leaders, observing from the parking lot to the pew and everywhere in between what guests might see. Review outdated bulletin boards to inadequate trash cans throughout the facility, and rank the issues from easiest to fix to the hardest. Tackle the low-hanging fruit and develop a long-term plan to solve the significant problems. Share what is being done weekly in your bulletin or announcements and celebrate when things get completed on the list. If a guest is sitting in the pew and hears this message on their first Sunday, they see/hear the action of the church coming back alive, and they might want to join in the efforts of reviving the declining church. The challenge will be to become more familiar with the list so that you remember to complete the list and constantly evaluate what needs to be added to the list over time.

Realize that the best days of the established church are not behind her but what lies before. Help your local church move from familiar to further preparing for guests so they feel welcomed, comfortable, and part of the family they want to join when they come. Be willing to change and see how the change enhances the church as part of the turnaround.

NO TURNING BACK: RENEWING THE COMMITMENT TO CHANGE

The local church sometimes is forced to say there is no turning back. No turning back and reviewing the glory days. No turning back in celebrating a pastor who has long since stood in the pulpit. No turning back to programs that would not work in today's context or neighborhood culture. It takes a no-turning-back leader to lead a church in the death throes of decline to bring it back to spiritual and numerical growth. The style of leadership is not foolhardy or for the faint of heart. The leader is a leader who is after God's own heart. Churches want to change, or at least they say as much when a pastor interviews. But there seems to be pushback when change comes to the person in power or position to help make change happen. Why? Because change is hard. Change is creating a new story. Change is challenging in how things have always been done within the power structure established over time within the inner workings of the church. The changing dynamic drastically redesigns the church from an inward focus to an outward posture. With change comes new ideas, programs, and people that only reinforce the change message on those who do not want to change.

The Clock Is Ticking

At the University of Chicago sits The Doomsday Clock. The clock is to remind humanity that we are closer and closer to extinction due to global crises. Inside the local church, there are ever-looming crises that many churches are aging, and the lack of community engagement is slowly killing the church's gospel effectiveness. Once the church was planted in the community as a beachhead against the world's sins, since that time it has become a gathering place for selected members to worship God and then go directly home, ignoring the plight right outside the doors.

Recently I spoke to a pastor of a church in the Midwest which is struggling to keep its doors open. The church has only nine remaining members, including the pastor and his spouse. When I reviewed his situation with him, I gave him the grim news that the church had less than six months to live unless significant but small changes were made to keep it open. With what could have been the church's last gasp of breath to stay alive, the pastor chose to begin implementing some of the changes as I agreed to work with him and the church for the next several months. This story is familiar. This scene is played out in silence regardless of denomination or location within North America. The church blames the pastor, the pastor blames the church, and the community is left to fend for itself with no gospel witness. If the church is going to move away from two minutes to midnight and not close its doors, then the church leadership must be willing to take the steps not to turn back the clock but to move forward into the God future before it.

Retool and Retrain

Churches who struggle say, "If we can just get a few young families, everything will be fine." While that might be a quick fix, it will not fix the long-term institutional change that must take place to reclaim God's mantle from the lay leaders. Evaluate what works and is not working throughout the church. If that seems too large of a task, limit it to the children's church or a defined program. Or the fellowship hall meals. Or whatever pressing area appears to be taking the church back into the past with little to no results. As you examine the program, begin to remove the good parts of the program or ministry and then retire the features that do not work. Why hang on to something that is broken or does not work in the current circumstances of the church? Retooling honors the past commitment and idea behind the ministry but prepares at the same time for the future and needs the church faces today.

As you retool programs, you will need to retrain staff or volunteers in a new way or how somebody should do it in the future. Warning! Prepare for the pushback; it will come. Ignore the negative hold-on-to-the-past comments and focus on the actions of a person saying that it's uncomfortable. Be cognizant that they still want to help but will need retraining in their area to carry out the new mission you have set out. If a person does not support the need for retooling and retraining, then a hard conversation should be had by both parties. The struggle is because the heart is willing, but the mind wants to hold to the traditions that challenge the changing season upon the local church community.

Wherever you find yourself as a leader in an established church, know this truth: you will not rebound overnight, as the church did not get into this situation overnight, but you can begin to use the clock to your advantage. Be a bold witness for Jesus that without real substantive change, the church will slowly die, and I do not think anyone wants that to be the church's legacy. Thinking back to my pastor friend in the Midwest, he did not make it. Health issues and a lack of clear direction did him in. Today, a new pastoral couple is at the helm, engaging the community and seeing fresh fruit.

Chapter 2

Prepare the Way
Getting Ready for Guests

Growing up in Florida I was constantly aware of the potential destruction of storms. Mainly from hurricane or tropical-force winds that could strike during a six-month period each year that we call hurricane season. It seems no part of the country is immune from destruction or as the insurance industry calls "acts of God." The established church has faced "acts of God" that have challenged her to the core. It fundamentally changes the way the church reacts to the changing circumstances that it faces. The time for doing nothing, hoping the changing season would pass, is not the reality that many churches including yours might be facing today. Change has come to the front door of the church. The pandemic-induced inflation has solidified that change is here to stay. So, what should a church do to embrace the change and to begin to prepare for the next season in the life of the church? The simple answer is, get ready for guests. Wallowing about what was does not help build the kingdom. It is time to turn the church's attention from grief to guests.

When you know a guest is coming to your house, I imagine you do your best to straighten up things, make sure it smells nice, and that everything is in its proper place, as you want to make a good impression. So too, in the life of the established church, her leadership should be preparing each week for guests to arrive. Let me pause, because I can already hear some of you say, "We have not had a guest for a long time!" But a guest could come this Sunday or next, and you must be ready. As the bride of Christ, the church is called to be ready for his return. The return of guests is coming to your local church, but are you ready to receive them?

WINNING THE "NEW" & "OLD" FRONT DOORS

Most likely, if you are reading this resource, you have either been the perspective candidate or a member of a board interviewing for a pastoral/church relationship. Inevitably the topic of church growth always comes up. Sometimes it is from the board looking at the prospective candidate as the silver bullet to the church's problem or the pastoral couple with children who will singlehandedly rebuild the children's and youth department. Ultimately the pastoral couple wants to be reassured that the local church desires real change. Either way, the growth topic is rightly examined in these early conversations. Each side of the relationship needs to know if they are willing to take the prayerful steps to move the church forward from a downward spiral into a position for God to help the church increase numerically and spiritually. Growth is more than just some fairy tale topic that is broached in an interview and never again. Rather it is one that leads to developing the infrastructure of the church to harness guests into members and members into disciple- makers who, in turn, invite more guests.

Decades ago, the church doors were where people would check out a local church. On rare occasions, maybe the church had a radio or small-market television ministry where non-members could connect to the church. But today, every church leader, through podcasts and social media availability, has a larger ministry footprint outside the geographical bounds of the church campus. So how does a church differentiate between the church down the street and them?

The simple yet complex answer is developing the infrastructure for sustained future growth that attracts guests to the church and keeps them when they arrive. When I write about attracting guests to the church, it is not through fog machines or concert-type services, unless that is your target population. I am speaking of creating a culture of excellence that values others and thus values the resources that God has bestowed upon your local church. Your local ministry is not just for the weekly attendees but for those who know of God but do not have a relationship with him.

Putting the words "all are welcome" on the church sign will not draw many guests through the doors. Personal relationships are crucial to turning an invitation into action and seeing the church begin to grow.

Winning the "New" Front Door

The pandemic taught the church that technology was not the enemy of the church but a friend of it. If technology is harnessed correctly, it could transform a local church from the mundane into a community-focused church. Nine times out of ten, guests will not just show up unsure of what to expect because they will have reviewed the church's website and social media pages looking for the flavor of your local church. Now don't get caught up on the word "flavor." But like Colonel Sanders, the founder of Kentucky Fried Chicken, seasoned his fried chicken with a secret combination of herbs and spices, there are secret ways that the church spices up its services. There are hundreds of different ways church is being done, even in your denomination. You might call it spices, flavors, or community context, but the worship styles and services are different. Foundationally, they are the same at the core, but how it is expressed locally can be a far cry from what it might have been three decades ago. In years past, people would show up and be unsure about what would happen. That time has come and gone.

Today, the guest wants to know the ins and outs of every portion of the service, right down to the expected dress code. It might sound silly in your local context, but in the broader Christian evangelical church, it is the reality and has become the new normal.

Websites and your social media pages are far more important than the church sign at the end of the driveway. If you are unsure about what matters, invite a friend who does not go to your church to review your media pages and listen to their thoughts. Remember that guests need to know the times, days, type of service, and the church's address. Each of these should be predominantly displayed on top of your media pages.

Winning the "Old" Front Door

Can we pause and admit that there is a battle for the souls of your community? The devil wants to discourage and dissuade your local church from becoming outward. But God plans to see the church leave the pews and go into the streets as servants. When guests pull into the parking lot, do they know how to enter the church building? While members learn where to go, do not assume a guest knows where to enter and exit the building. In older churches, there are typically multiple entrances. Is there signage that suggests the main entrance? Are there parking lot greeters that can direct a guest? Are there friendly door greeters that open the door with a warm smile and a friendly hello? It might seem basic, but doing basics well leaves a lasting expression of a church that cares.

Guests are entering unfamiliar territory, and they need guidance. The guest has left the car, and they walk into the lobby, foyer, or narthex; is there someone there to guide them to the next steps? Possibly finding their child's classroom, the education wing to attend a Sunday school class, or being shown into the sanctuary. Have someone there to support and help your guests transition from the front door to the family of God. At this stage, every interaction is essential. You might not realize it, but guests judge the church on the quality of interactions, helpfulness in the way of signage, cleanliness of facilities, and overall appearance. Remember, this is all before even the pastor has preached a word or a song has been sung. Win the "old" front door by renewing the church's commitment to winning every interaction from the moment a guest pulls into the parking lot until they leave.

Winning the new and old front doors is more than just sprucing up the place. It is reconnecting the church's love for guests and current members, melding them into one family of God.

DEVELOPING THE INFRASTRUCTURE FOR THE FUTURE

Regardless of church size, churches have learned that technology and ministry are inextricably linked together. Once, the church could advertise in traditional ways (newspaper ads, radio spots, and a church sign), and people would come to the church for special services or weekly gatherings, but that model of passive evangelism has changed. The church has slowly adapted to the changing reality, while the population has leaned into technology through smartphones, tablets, and other devices for several decades. However, the pandemic forced many established churches to find creative ways to see technology as a tool to enhance their services to reach the community.

Technology Connects the Community with the Church

For many churches, the neighborhood has radically changed, and they have failed to connect regularly with their neighbors and thus have slowly declined. For decades the church could open its doors, and the community would flock to it. As churches have leaned into technology, they have learned that the new front door is the church's website, where community members review them before they attend a service. A well-designed website that addresses guests' questions, such as the church's physical address, service times, dress code, expectations of service, and childcare, to name a few, enhances the prospect of hosting guests weekly.

Technology Enhances the Worship Experience

In early 2020, as the pandemic set in, churches leaned into streaming to broadcast their services. Many needed the technology but needed to learn how to use it. They found a way to share their services through smartphones and free social media platforms. Over time, they have seen the value of having specialized equipment to enhance the quality of broadcast, sound, and experience. However, many churches still need direction and help to improve the worship experience. Through online tithing, QR codes to capture guests' information, easy and fast check-in for kids, and a one-stop location for social media for guests to view the services are needed. As the church faces the new frontier, technology can help the local church connect better with guests and regular members.

Technology Supports the Mission

Technology is not a fad for local churches but will become the hub for spreading the gospel message. Throughout the centuries, the church has had to adapt to the changing dynamics that the culture has placed upon them. This decade is no different. The pandemic has helped the church realize that the mission should be lived out more than Sunday. The church has found a new voice through technology to use resources such as audio and video podcasts to share the gospel relationally while propelling the local church's mission forward, allowing technology to be used daily through online gatherings for Bible studies, meetings, and counseling sessions. The church's mission has not changed, but the advent of radio, television, and now the internet and the technology developed around it has enhanced the broadcast of the mission like never before.

Instead of fearing technology as in the past, churches have embraced the new way forward to expand their mission, as a local church called to reach their community and beyond.

TOMORROW IS SET BY WHAT THE CHURCH DOES TODAY

What you do today is as important as what you might do tomorrow. In 2 Kings chapter 2, we read about the prophet Elijah walking with his understudy Elisha. Elijah was preparing to go home to be with the Lord, and Elisha wanted to make sure the mantle of Elijah fell on him, so he stayed ever close. Much like Elisha, the church must wish to remain so close to God and his plans for the local church that the church people move with him when he moves. But sadly, far too many churches and their leaders are moving in the direction of comfort, not God's. When you look at your local church, where is the mantle of the church? Is the church stuck in the 1970s or '80s as an elaborate museum of the past? That is not where God is; he is in today and tomorrow. As a leader, you are called to be like Elisha, who is desperate to see God move, so much so that you would stay close to him in your prayer, preaching, and participation time. When Elijah was taken into heaven, Elisha claimed the mantle of Elijah and would see more signs and wonders than his teacher. A double-portion blessing had fallen on him. The established church has a second and third act of her life if she is willing to stay close to God and obey his commands. But it takes a leader like you to get out of God's way and begin following him.

Recently I went on the website of a church that runs at over 600 people in weekly attendance. The website was something out of the early 2000s. It was antiquated and hard to navigate. If I were a guest, I would instantly see that they were stuck in a time warp of a past era, making me pause. Why? Because people want a church that is alive, not half-baked and on its way to death. You may say, "Well, the church must be doing something right because of its size"—yet it's not preparing for the future, as most of the congregation is older. Without tweaking the foundation's outer edges, the foundation will not stand under the weight of deaths that will come with age. Like Elisha, the church must become hungry for guests. That takes the church developing an infrastructure for future guests. Your website, social media pages, podcast, signage (inside and outside the church), room design, etc., speaks volumes to the church's values.

In 2 Kings 2:19(NIV), "The men of the city said to Elisha, 'Look, our lord, this town is well situated, as you can see, but the water is bad, and the land is unproductive.'" The town was there, but the infrastructure for sustained future growth needed to be improved. Just because you have people today does not mean you ignore what may happen ten years later. You have an obligation to redesign and instill the infrastructure that will help your local church become productive well into the future.

Care for the Facility with Guest's Eyes

Elisha asked the men telling him the ground and water were unproductive, to bring him a new bowl. In essence, he said, let's look at this problem with fresh eyes. Gather with a group of members who are willing to see the church change to reach its neighbors. This small group should be ready to critically evaluate all aspects of the church from the inside out. Much like laying the groundwork for a new street or neighborhood, the church has to envision where things should go and how things should come in the future. One small example of developing infrastructure is your guest's information card. What is the purpose? If the intention is to gather and share information, is the card streamlined enough to accomplish that task? Guests do not want to feel like they are filling out an application for a loan to attend your church. Make sure it asks for basic limited information that somebody can glean and plug the person or family into ministries in the church. The church should not use the guest's card to collect details that the church will never use. One way my local church uses a subliminal message through the guest information card is to list five service organizations that we invest in as part of our mission at the bottom of the guest card. We share that if a guest fills out the card when spoken about from the stage during the service and circles one of the five organizations, we will donate $5.00 in their name to that agency of their choice. By adding value to the guest card, we are saying to the guest we not only value you for showing up and the information you are filling out, but we value the partner agencies we get to partner with as a church. Place value where value needs to be placed and eliminate all unnecessary distractions.

Create Easy On-Ramps

Do not make it difficult for a guest to find your church. Ensure your website has your physical address, telephone number, and other essential information at the very top of the page. Far too many church websites hide that information in a tab or at the bottom of the page. Guests do not want to search for basic information. They want it quick and fast. Look at your website and social media pages as if you were a guest. Have selected ages within your church go to these sites and provide honest and open feedback. Make sure you do not leave out any age. If you do not have children in your church, ask your grandchild or a neighborhood teen to do so because their feedback will be valuable to the church's future. It would help if you had a plethora of feedback to enhance what you are already doing to capture guests.

Review all materials that guests may touch:

- Bulletins: These should be designed with the guests in mind, not members. For instance, information about the next potluck should have enough information that guests would know where to go, what to bring, and how to get there. Information placed weekly in the bulletin should be about sharing the church's values, not just information for members. Be honest with yourself; guests do not care how much money the church has brought in weekly, how many people attended last week compared to the previous year, or the names on the prayer list, as they most likely do not know anyone. What they do care about is the order of service, the next activity they could join, and where to find the pastor/church office number if they need something during the week.

- Announcements: Less is better. If the announcement is in the bulletin, has been shared on social media, or a slide before service, why does a guest or a member want someone to read what they have already read themselves? Yet, announcements are as crucial as offerings in some churches. Announcements were made in churches many decades ago because most people could not read. Today we have a high literacy rate in churches. Only announce the important stuff, not everything the church is doing. Develop instead a monthly newsletter that can be mailed or emailed to members if you want to share announcements at greater length.

- Greeters: During the pandemic, we heard a lot about essential workers. Greeters are the church's front-line essential workers who can leave a positive or negative impression on guests. One sour greeter can ruin the church for a potential attendee, so make sure greeters are trained in customer service to welcome, guide, and have a conversation with first-time guests.

These highlighted areas are only a small handful of what should be reviewed as you look at on-ramps for first-time guests.

Connect through Varying Avenues

Once a guest comes several weeks in a row, what then? Find creative ways to get them plugged into the church culture. Ask them if they would like to help pass out bulletins, serve coffee, or be a door greeter. Think about all the frontline opportunities for people to serve. Be cognizant that they should not be put in positions of authority or overseeing children but placed in areas where they can feel they are part of a family and not just an outsider. Over the last number of years in my local church, there has been a significant shift in leadership from those serving for decades to newcomers. This shift has created excitement for the newcomers that they feel part of something larger than themselves, while the long-term members can see the value of newer people coming to the church. Some long-term members have felt pushed out or rejected when new members have come into positions of service, which has caused friction. But you cannot allow the negative mindset of some to hold back the church from growing forward in a new Christ direction.

Finding ways for newcomers to serve is like restoring the wells that needed to be more productive in Elisha's time. As Elisha was brought a new bowl (2 Kings 2:20), Elisha put salt in the bowl and then went out to well and threw it upon the waters. "This is what the Lord says, 'I have healed this water. Never again will it cause death or make the land unproductive'" (2 Kings 2:21). By obeying God and preparing the church for future guests by evaluating and then enhancing the church's infrastructure, you are making what once was dead and bringing it back to life. Trust the God process and allow God to help transform the old into the new.

CREATING A POSITIVE GUEST EXPERIENCE

Recently traveling in the Florida Everglades, my family and I stopped at a roadside attraction that took us back to when Florida residents lived at a slower pace. Like the established church, which has seen better days, this attraction had an old-world charm, like stepping back in a time warp. One of the high-walled exhibits along the crushed-shelled walk with a fence around it had a sign that read "turtles," yet inside the enclosure were alligators. The identification sign and the actual message were two different things. Today, there are conflicting messages that churches are putting out, saying they want guests, but they are not preparing or even acting like they want them to attend. This small lesson of the wrong sign with the wrong attraction reminds us that the church's message to the outside world should not conflict with the inside experience of a guest.

Make Sure the Message and the Method Match

The sign on the exhibit reminded me of a bait and switch that many churches unintentionally use on potential guests. For instance, on the church's website, a church might use stock photos of diverse people and families with children, and then when a guest arrives, finds the congregation less diverse and has no children. Ensure the message the church shares on its website, social media pages, and in-person equals the experience guests will encounter when they arrive. In days gone by, people would check out a church by showing up; now, they pull up social media pages to see what the church offers. Today potential guests will review all media avenues to "see" before they "attend" the local church, so make sure the message and the method match.

Think about your local church this way. What message are the church's media pages sending to prospective guests? What needs to be changed or positively highlighted to let future guests know more about the church? The thought and work you put into this area will help your church retain more guests, as the guests will already know what to expect when they arrive.

Create a Community of Care for Guests

When a guest walks into the foyer (lobby or narthex) for the first time, what will they experience? Guests are looking for directions and connections. Ensure there is someone there who not only opens the door with a friendly smile for them but provides recommendations for the next steps. If the family has children, let them know where the children check-in is or where their classroom might be. Better yet, walk them over, help them check in their children, and point out the restrooms or other areas you feel they need to know about as you interact with them. Help your guests feel welcomed and valued as part of their visit. Sadly, a few door greeters do a great job greeting but leave a guest alone. Follow through to create a community of care for guests by caring for them from the moment they enter the foyer until they leave.

Think about the next steps as a guest comes into the foyer. Do you have a person or a team of people to help direct, guide, and provide the answers to the questions that guests might have? Can someone walk them through check-in for children, show them to the sanctuary, and invite them to sit next to them so they have a community connection right away? This could be an excellent place for the friendliest people inside your church to minister and to reinforce to a guest that your church cares about their visit.

Focus on First Impressions

Ask yourself, why do we want guests to come to the church? While the answer might be obvious to some, ensure every member knows the local church's mission. In a post-Christian world, the church has difficulty connecting with marginalized Christians and non-Christians in the community as never before. The church's goal is gospel connections, but many established churches focus on connecting with members and forgetting about future guest connections. You have probably heard the statement; first impressions are lasting impressions. What must you do to make a positive first impression if that is the case? Some of the primary things that a guest will look for is signage. Is there updated clear signage for guests entering the church building, as many established churches have multiple entrances? Once guests enter the foyer, ensure signage directs them to the sanctuary, restrooms, classrooms, guests' check-in, etc., and it's big enough to be seen from across the room and not just up close as a guest will scan the room looking for next steps if a church member has not helped them.

Review the building with guests' eyes, remove outdated material, and replace torn or well-worn furniture, carpets, and signage. Paint and update high-traffic areas. Clean out the backs of the pews and remove any debris from last week's service while observing what guests might see on the platform from where they might sit, as the church's goal is to provide a clean and welcoming space for guests. When you position the church through guests' eyes, these little steps will have a big payoff.

Follow Up the Fellowship with Personal Touches

After a guest visits the church for the first time, how do you follow up with them? Develop steps that continue to create connections with first-time guests by developing a four-step process.

Step 1. Get contact information.

Ensure your connection card asks for basic information such as name, address, email address, phone number, and if they receive text messages. The goal is to connect with a person in the future, not to explore their life history, so keep the connection cards simple.

Step 2: Connect during the week twice.

Send a letter signed by the pastor with a handwritten note that thanks them for coming. On Saturday, have someone from the church office call or text, inviting them back to church the next day.

Step 3: Member connects.

During the second week after the first visit, a member from the greeting team could send a handwritten card thanking the person for attending and inviting them back to an upcoming event at the church.

Step 4: Saturday night call or text.

It has now been two weeks since the first visit and the fourth contact from the church. Have a different member from the greeting team call or text on Saturday night inviting the person back to church.

    These are a few ways to get the church ready for guests. In a disconnected world, these steps provide tangible connection points between the church and guests, letting them know the church values their visit. If a church is proactive, guests will see the care put in place, and the church will win more first-time guests' overtime than lose.

Chapter 3

Welcome Home
Reimagine the Space

For decades churches were built with the mindset that bigger is better. The "If you build it, they will come" mentality took hold with the church growth movement of the 1980s and '90s. Since that time the Christian church has shifted to smaller gatherings and more intimate settings. The COVID pandemic exposed the facility of what once worked decades ago will not work today. Once massive worship centers where guests were able to hide among the faithful have been replaced with intimate spaces dedicated to drawing people together. While the footprint size of these half- empty churches has not changed, the people have. Where once Christians and those seeking the Lord flocked to opened church doors. Today the church stands as a monument to that past philosophy. Hear my heart, I am not condemning the church-growth movement, because clearly for many churches God moved in a mighty way, but I am cautioning the era of "bigger is better" is over.

REDEEMING THE SPACE FOR GUESTS

As weekly attendance has decreased for many established churches, it has become more apparent that the church building is no longer conducive to what the church needs today. Any change brings pushback for some and for still others positive excitement about what is coming. It depends on which side of the fence you are viewing the shift. Throughout Scripture, you read about men and women who sought change, not for change's sake, but to redeem what God had initially birthed. So too today, the church is still called to adapt and move forward into the present future God has for the local church. Change, while scary, can be rewarding if the church is willing to redeem spaces for guests that are currently underutilized or not at all.

Reclaim the Past and Bring It into the Future

The campus of the local church is ripe with history. With such a rich history comes fiefdoms who hold onto past practices, room assignments, and furniture that become small idols within the church. When redeeming a space to prepare for the future, a leader must navigate the minefield of the glory days to reclaim what God wants to do today.

While the footprint of a traditional church building does not have to change, the inside workings, from room designations to the sanctuary's design, might have to change to fit the new ideas and new era that the church has entered. Instead of thinking about the church as "mine," begin to look at the church as a place of "yet to be." The yet to be is what is to come. The local church can still celebrate the past but be focused on the present needs by preparing for the future. In one of the churches I served in, we reclaimed a small hallway to turn it into a museum of the past. We placed plaques, pictures, etc., in this space to honor who we had been but redesigned the inside of the church footprint by turning classrooms into a coffee house and a mission center where we collected and packed items for missional outreach programs. Let me challenge you to be creative with your current space by being Christ to the people inside the church, knowing change is not easy, but always look towards what guests or the community needs outside the church and dream of what could be in the redesigned space.

Repair to Present a Good Face Forward

When you see the local church through guests' eyes and not just as a regular member, you begin to see the church's needs. How often have you or the local church prayed for guests who come and do not stay? Is it because you did not prepare the church for guests? Sometimes it is about cleaning a classroom or taking away items from the foyer to prepare for the guests who will come. As you begin reviewing your current space, you will likely see things you have become accustomed to over time. Deferred maintenance issues will come to the forefront, and a plan must be devised to begin to tackle the problems. Deferred maintenance in older church buildings is not new and should be dealt with in a fashion that prioritizes quick fixes to complex problems. Having a plan is the first step, but the project must be acted upon and not debated for all eternity. By dividing up the repair plan, you can lessen the overwhelming list of small jobs that can be tackled with the right resources and actions.

Think about it this way: If a guest were coming to your home, you would probably begin to straighten things up, clean out the cobwebs from the corners of the room, dust, throw out trash, and move items that don't belong. It is preparing for the guests that will come through your doors and being ready to welcome them with a clean, organized facility that is in good repair.

Restore What Has Been Lost

As an established church, the church has faced a lot of losses over the years. Losses can be seen as a lack of attendance, decreased giving, fewer children, and lack of community engagement, but through it all, God has remained. Have you ever asked yourself; why have I stayed through all the change? Most likely, it has been because of God. God has called you and the people around you to the church location you serve. It is not by accident but by divine appointment that God has kept you in a place of such challenge. Yet, in the challenging season, God is still working. As you begin to view the church campus as a connecting point (jump-off point) for community engagement, you begin to see where God is challenging your leadership to step up and out of its spiritual comfort zone to reach the loss of the community.

The God you serve is a *big* God. Not a small-minded; forget about you, God. Trust him and yourself as you lead the people forward in restoring what has been lost.

Retire Programs That Don't Fit Today's Vision

Do you have enough people to run the programs you currently have listed in the directory? Most likely not, and your church is not alone. Instead of offering a programmatic cafeteria-style listing for everyone, focus on what you can do well to reach the most people. That may mean that programs that were successful twenty-five years ago will have to be retired, and those resources of people and funding are put into a new area. Focus on what the church has and evaluate if it meets the community's needs. If it does not, then the church needs to pivot by placing resources where God can make the most use of what the church has.

As programs are retired, it is an opportunity to celebrate what God has done through the church in the past. Highlight people who have helped lead the programs in the past to let them know what they have done has brought value to the kingdom as the church celebrates its history, layout the new program, and leaders who will lead the programs in the future. Have the former programmatic leaders pray over the new leaders to show the continuity of service to the local church and the broader community. Remember that yesterday matters as much as today. Still, the future is always ahead. By retiring programs that no longer fit today's culture, you begin to extend the community to another generation through slight modifications and programs that reach today's Christ followers.

Renew Your Commitment to Reaching Neighbors

There was a time that the church could open its doors three times a week, and the parking lot would be filled with families driving in. Today, many churches have no young families, and fewer and fewer people are driving into her parking lot. Even amid decline, there is hope found in Christ. You cannot go back and change yesterday, but you can begin again today. Renew the church's commitment to reach your neighbors by finding out the needs of those around you and moving towards addressing those needs.

Outside the walls of the established church is a community that is all but forgotten. The church was once a part of their lives, but they do not know who the neighbors are today. By reconnecting through listening, learning the needs, and addressing the community needs with the church's neighbors, you will bring the church back to the forefront of what has been missing, which is a deep community connection.

Guests can move to become members if the church is willing to redeem its current space for the future needs of the community. Redeeming the church's footprint for guests is not a new program or a quick fix. It is a a partnership with God and his people inside and outside the church, to live like Christ not just on Sundays but throughout the week with the church and her neighbors walking together, that is a long-term fix.

THE ERA OF THE BIG CHURCH IS OVER

While the church would like to believe that the size of a congregation does not matter, it matters to leaders across all denominational lines with deadly spiritual consequences. Recently a pastoral colleague was turned down from submitting his resume to a church because, in their words, "he did not qualify because he was pastoring a small church." Another pastoral friend was turned down from a church because he lived in a rural part of the country, and the search committee did not think he could minister in an urban setting even though he currently has a church of over 300 in average weekly attendance.

According to a recent Lifeway Research survey, "7 in 10 U.S. churches have 100 or fewer weekly worship service attendees, while 7 in 10 U.S. churchgoers attend a church with more than 250 each week. Half of all churches have fewer than 65 people in their weekly worship service."[1] The era of the big church is over! The idea is that bigger is better, urban is better, is the wrong mindset for denominational leaders, clergy, and congregational members. The only size that matters is a one-on-one personal relationship with Jesus Christ. So why do denominational leaders, church search committees, and boards refuse to recognize that a pastor with the right skillsets which fits the local context can pastor a church of five or 500? If the pandemic has taught the Christian church anything, it's that God can use any person, any size church, to expand the gospel. All he needs is a willing vessel.

Worship Size Matters More for Self-Esteem than Relationship to God

If you are a pastor, I want you to ask yourself, *Why do I serve in my current assignment?* I imagine you did not say, *So that I could earn a paycheck.* Because believe me, there are many easier ways to serve at a traditional nine-to-five job, with better compensation and retirement plans, than pastoring a local church. Yet far too many pastors feel ineffective because of the number of people attending service each week. The reality is that the church has a self-esteem issue more than a worship issue. Nowhere in Scripture can

---

1. Aaron Earls, "22 Vital Stats for Ministry in 2022," *Lifeway Research*, January 5, 2022 (para. 28), https://research.lifeway.com/2022/01/05/22-vital-stats-for-ministry-in-2022/.

I find Jesus' remarking on church size. But he is seen several times speaking of the spiritual effectiveness of the leaders. Pastor, your worth is not found in if you can build a crowd. Your effectiveness is found in each soul surrendered to God as you serve where he has called you. The idea that bottoms in the seat are more important than souls surrendered to God is wrong.

God sees your work. He hears your prayers. He grieves when you grieve. He celebrates when you celebrate. He never said to gather a crowd of five thousand and be a megachurch pastor, and you retain a special place in heaven. No! He called you to be effective right where you are. Rural or urban. Small or large. All he wants is for you to serve him and share the story of redemption with those you meet. If your church grows because of it, then great, but that should not be the leader or church's driving force. Focus on God and keep the main thing the main thing: a relationship with Jesus Christ.

Worship Size Matters to Others More than the Attendee

Most pastors have walked into a half-empty sanctuary to preach. For most pastors in the United States, that is a weekly occurrence. While there might be outliers who have shared the thought that this is a "small church," most attendees never have it cross their minds. If they were looking for size, they certainly would not go to more than 70 percent of churches in the United States. Guests coming to your local church most likely come because someone invited them. They are not looking for programs but for people who will love them. A pastor who will shepherd them. And a God who will renew them. There is a negative mindset that a smaller church is ineffective, that the pastor and its leaders have failed God or at least mismanaged his resources. That, my friend, is a lie sent straight from hell. God values the local church, and more importantly, he loves the people who make up the church.

The era of bigger is better has been left in the last decade. A new generation of Christians is seeking the age of neighborhood churches and the restoration of the established church. New Christians are not seeking programs; they seek people who live on mission. The local church can be made up of ten people and still be effective by serving at a local elementary school by tutoring students or adopting a classroom. The Christian Church in North America needs to be on a mission, winning the lost and loving their neighbors more than gathering the largest group of people each week.

Worship Size Does Not Matter to God

Each week I attend Kiwanis, a social club dedicated to serving children. Everything we do is to focus on our mission of helping children. Weekly our club averages fifteen people, yet we volunteer over a thousand hours yearly by serving in forty-eight activities, all aimed at benefiting children. Now, look at your church. Refrain from telling yourself that you cannot help because you have fewer than twenty people. No. If you have more than two, God is with you, which means the church can do something. I do not believe God looks at your church weekly and puts the worship attendance number or even the offering number on his number board in heaven. So why does your church? You do it because it is what the church has always done. What if what you have always done needs to be fixed? Change! Change your thinking to change your habits.

Your worth as a pastor or local church is not found in the numbers but in what those numbers represent. Each number you are counting is counted not for a tally sheet but for a heart won or lost in a relationship with God. Be obedient to God and love the people around you. Find ways to invest in a person or a family's life. Do acts of service not for a reward to build your church but to serve God's church.

Wherever you find yourself today, do not find your worth or call in how many people sit and listen to a sermon each Sunday. The life you live outside the church might be far more important than the one that shows up on Sunday morning because non-Christians are watching you in your workplace, at the grocery store, or eating at a restaurant. You can dress up on Sunday and play church and not be as effective as you can be in being Christ to all. Challenge yourself to be Christ always, in all ways, and focus on what matters, serving God and living out your call daily.

RETHINKING THE CHURCH FOOTPRINT

The hustle and bustle of the church, growing fast and filled with families, has all but dried up. You sense in your spirit the church that once had families is declining. As you look over the property, you see deferred maintenance, empty classrooms where once children's laughter filled the space, and the clutter that now overflows a room where once adults had a Bible study. The once massive church footprint has now become an albatross around the neck of many established churches, a shell of her former self.

I have heard it often said, "If we could find the right pastor with the right experience but still young enough to attract families, we would grow again." Or "If we could just have one or two families from one of the larger churches in town, we would begin to grow." Over time that mindset has brought forth a spirit of discouragement. The remaining members are resigned that the church will die with their generation but still do their best to hold on. This large, empty church image is being played out in towns and cities nationwide. One must ask, is God dead? Is Christianity dead? Is the church doomed? Surely not! God still has a plan for your church.

Instead of seeing the picture as unfavorable, why not begin to see that God has not forgotten your church? Sure, the signs of defeat are everywhere, but where there are two, Christ is in the midst. One sure way to die is to do nothing, but in doing something, even if you fail, the church will go down with a fight instead of slowly drifting into death.

Rethink the Outside View of the Church

What is the image that the community has of your church? Begin to change that image by reimagining the church from the parking lot to the pew and everywhere in between. Begin to scan what the parking lot and church campus might say to the potential visitor. As the visitor certainly will, you might notice that the clear lines of parking spaces have faded with time. The once-smooth asphalt has weeds protruding through its cracks, exposing the lack of maintenance. Observing the building in the morning sun, you can see it bleached and faded, revealing the well-worn church sign beckoning guests and attendees alike to enter. What if, instead of doing nothing, you begin to do something? Begin to reimage the car-filled space; families exiting their vehicles heading for the church, doors of the main entrance open by trained greeters who gladly welcome guests and church members alike.

As you picture that image in your mind, begin to strategize what steps should be taken to see that image go from a dream into reality. While the church might not be able to afford a newly paved parking lot, it can afford a can of weed killer and a lawn mower that can cut down the overgrown grass protruding from the cracks in the lot. Where worn lines expose old parking spots, the church can paint new lines at a fraction of the cost of hiring a firm. When looking across the parking lot are there sheds, small buildings, or picnic shelters that need to be taken down, or at least spruced up? As you look over the lot, you may see trees that need to be removed or bushes trimmed back. Is there an old fence that needs some loving care? How about old playground equipment or an old ball field that has seen better days? Do not be overwhelmed at all the work that needs to be done but realize that small and large things distract from the overall mission of serving God locally, and your role is to remove as many distractions as possible. Little by little, by tackling these projects you can begin to enhance the grounds that God has called you to steward.

As you stand back and admire the work, you might notice that the building has peeling paint, and you gather a team to begin to paint the building one weekend at a time, and before you know it, the outside of the building is fully painted. With the parking lot and building returning to life, you now focus on updating the signage, so the community will notice that life is being brought back to the run-down building. Where once despair took hold, it has been replaced with hope. All it takes is a willing heart to do something.

Rethink the Inside Use and Space of the Church

As you step into your lobby, what do you see? Many struggling churches will see celebrations from the past. Memorial walls, plaques, and trophies from past victories form a quasi-mausoleum to the church's history instead of creating a space welcoming a new visitor. In a day when less is more, the church says more stuff is more. Please hear my heart. I do not want to ignore or forget the past, but the church should honor the past, present, and future by creating spaces more conducive to the needs.

Members must remember that the church is not their home. It is not a member's desire or likes that should decorate the church. Anything such as plastic flowers, awards, or _____ (you fill in the blank) that distracts from the mission of welcoming guests should be removed and put in a place that honors the past and the present needs. The campus and, by extension, the church lobby is an extension of the House of God; thus, it should be a place that honors the view of reaching people with the gospel of Christ.

As you move from the lobby into a hallway, turn your attention to the classrooms that have become storage rooms. What does this say to guests? Initially, it tells the guests it was not prepared for them, and their children. Begin combing these hidden treasure troves of collected material and process what can be used now and what might need to be donated. Realizing that a church cannot keep everything it has collected over the years, it should be reviewed for use today or discarded with care as it has outlived its usefulness. While this will be one of the most challenging tasks to accomplish and will be fraught with emotion, remember that the church is preparing for future families and children, and therefore you must make room for what God will do next. What you see today is not what God wants you to do in the future. Begin to see the needs outside of your current situation and as you move towards completing God's dream for the property, he will bless the work of your hands.

These two steps do not address the worship center, restrooms, fellowship hall, children's areas, etc., but they give you an idea that change is hard. If the church rebounds from decline, it must decide to live. Will you choose to lead the change that lets the church live? Will you help your church see that changing things is not for change's sake but a step in rebounding from decline back to life? God did not call you to this assignment so you would bury the church but to help revive the church. As you reimagine the space, God will provide the vision to accomplish the goal and help bring the church back to life.

TURN THE NEGATIVE IMAGE OF THE CAMPUS INTO A POSITIVE ONE

As you wander around the campus, the echoes of what the church used to be speaks to your soul. Where families and children filled the empty spaces, today, you hear the shuffling of feet from the current members, a reminder of what has changed throughout the decades. The leadership at the church realizes that the church building and property may be too large for current needs and wonders what the church should do. Here are five options that I would encourage you and your church leadership team to review.

Option 1: Do Nothing

Change is difficult in the most desirable circumstances. But change in a low season is almost impossible without a robust and determined group of leaders who want to see the church live again. If a church chooses to stay stagnant and waits on someone to show up without doing their part, then nothing will happen. Nothing plus nothing equals, well, nothing. Yes, you read that right. When the church leadership does nothing, nothing happens. When the church's culture is nothing, God rewards the church with nothing. Over time, a nothing mindset will slowly destroy the church until nothing is left.

Option 2: Share the Property

Most church properties are used three times a week (Sunday morning, Sunday night, and Wednesday night) for four to six hours weekly. For most of the week, the building and grounds are underutilized. Have you ever thought about sharing your property with another church or ministry? When I pastored in Louisville, Kentucky, the church had too much space and few people to fill it, so we decided to share facilities with an Independent African American church and a Hispanic congregation. Working together, we lowered the cost for everyone by sharing resources split three ways. In time this partnership strengthened each of our congregations and provided vibrancy to the property. Another way to see the blessing was, instead of three rooms filled with fake flowers to decorate the church, it became one, and the two others became an office for one of the churches and a Sunday school classroom for all three churches to use.

Option 3: Rent the Property

In previous decades, a church was built for size; today, they are built for ministry. With land prices increasing over time, selling and buying/building elsewhere is not cost-effective for smaller, struggling churches. Have you considered finding a smaller location that your church can rent so you may rent out the larger church campus to a thriving church while holding a long-term lease on the original property? A positive cash flow for your smaller church venue will enable your church to save money over time and reinvest in your rented church facility, original campus, or a new outreach ministry.

If your church grows in the rented location and needs more space, the church can always move back into the former main campus at the end of the rental agreement with the leasing church. If your church decides to stay at the rented facility long-term, you can renew the long-term lease on the original church-owned property or sell the land to the current renters. Either way, you have developed a cash flow that will continue to help the church far into the future.

Option 4: Sell the Property

When the church was built, no one could imagine you might have to sell it someday. Over the decades, the lack of maintenance, the aging population, and poor community engagement led the church to sell the property. Think about it this way. What if selling the current facility to another church or commercial developer gives the local church a new lease on life? What if a new location, facility, and community focus is like a heart transplant that provides the body with life for decades? Instead of fearing change, the church can lean into the transition by recalibrating the church's ministry vision with the new reality by using the new lease on life to recapture God's focus.

Option 5: Recreate the Property

For far too long, members have allowed the past to dictate the future when all the church needed to do to live again was to evolve with the times and community around them. Evolve programs, rooms, and empty spaces into new ministry opportunities to reach the community. Instead of looking at the physical footprint of the church with dread, see it as an opportunity to reimage the space with new ministry opportunities in mind. One classroom that used to have children has become a room filled with "stuff" that no one had the heart to throw out. Instead of having more closets, why not turn the classroom into a computer room as part of a new after-school program in partnership with a local elementary school, or turn one empty parking lot into a new basketball court for the community to use when the church is not in session?

Recreating is not ending the church. It is redesigning your current space with the original mission in mind, to win people to Jesus. Do not allow fear to control the church's faith. Dream again! Believe again! Live for Jesus again!

Chapter 4

Be the One
Investing in Relationships

How are you? It is a simple question that reveals a lot when you ask a leader in the church that question. Leaders have faced the challenge of a pandemic and people not returning to the local church. They have been dealt spiritual body blows when a long-term member leaves the church and cites the leaders' preaching and teaching as lacking. Understandably, ministry creates change—just the nature of the calling makes a change—but change is hard when a pastor has poured everything into the local church only to be or feel rejected. With change, from a lack of attendance to low offerings, the pastor-leader faces more questions about whether they should move on or stay put in their current assignment.

Leaders today are facing discouragement and questioning if they will continue in their ministry assignment or ministry altogether. In a hard season, one must remember that there is a harvest just around the corner if the leader is willing to stick to God's calling and do ministry work.

Keep Tilling the Soil

Why is ministry so hard? Where are all the people? Who is going to serve in the necessary positions in the church? These and other questions have been asked of me as a pastor who serves in the established church. I have had to realize that ministry has never been easy. Even before Christ walked this earth, it has been hard to share the gospel and live it out. However, God has called you to keep tilling the soil. Tilling can look like starting a small group Bible study, sharing a meal once a week with neighbors on your street, being an encourager in the workplace, or donating your time to a nonprofit.

As a leader, you work the ground (your current members, neighbors, workplace employees, etc.) that you have now and trust God to bring new members out of what you do today. Like a summer garden, it is in late fall that the ground is fertilized and tilled one last time before springtime preparations, which will come after a long, cold winter. Tilling is about preparing; your harvest will come when you prepare the spiritual ground for future guests and your current members to grow spiritually.

Keep Praying for Lost Souls

How is your prayer life? That one question struck me as odd but profound when my mentor asked it. How about you? How is your prayer life? You are busy praying for others as a leader, but what about your needs? Prayer must not be a two- or three-minute part of a service but ongoing communication with Christ daily. Everyone you encounter can be part of your prayer movement throughout the day. Prayer is essential to stem the tide of discouragement and sows seeds for a future harvest. Prayer must be more than just a ritual; it must become a habit exercised daily.

God has people in the places you visit throughout the week that need a relationship with him. But far too many people are so busy living life that they are missing the essential ingredient for their spiritual life, a relationship with Jesus. Begin to pray daily for opportunities to live out your faith. Ask God to open the door to connect as you meet random strangers. Use these "chance moments" as God moments where you can impact a stranger's life. Pray for these God -moments before you leave the car and enter a store. Pray that God would lead you to encourage or support a person in need as you walk around. Sometimes we think it has to be a program for it to be effective, when all God is asking us to do is live our life like Jesus. Pray, seek, love, give, and share your faith.

Keep Preparing for the Harvest to Come

As you begin to walk more comfortably in your faith, understand that there may be seasons of dryness where you do not see fruit from the seeds that are being planted. Let me encourage you to keep pressing on. The harvest that God has for your ministry will come in God's timing, so stay faithful. Stay prayed up. Stay focused on reaching the lost, one personal interaction at a time. I have often wondered how much of the harvest I missed because I became complacent and forgot to keep preparing for it.

Pastoring an established church celebrating eighty years of life a few years ago, I was constantly looking for new ways to freshen up the church's footprint to be a welcoming place for guests. From an indoor trick-or-treat to transforming a classroom into a coffee shop, the space God had given was adapted to meet the current season. Let me encourage you, instead of being discouraged at what the church does not have, begin to dream about what can be in the space you have and prepare for the harvest to come.

Keep Being Faithful

A mentor shared seven words that radically changed my ministry a decade ago; I believe it can impact you also. "You are doing better than you realize." Leader, remember you are leading well. You are leading like Jesus. Do not give in to the negative voice in your head or the person in the pew. Focus on the main thing. Keep preaching and relationally teaching the gospel. Stay focused on living out the gospel one conversation or service at a time. Be faithful in season and out of season.

Think about it this way: how many people, pastors, and churches have missed the harvest because they gave up too soon? God has amazing plans for your ministry and the life of your church if you are willing to plod along doing the work to prepare for what is to come. There will be days of great joy and deep disappointment, but through it all, know God sees you, hears your prayers, and is preparing a harvest to come.

BECOMING A CONNECTOR CHURCH

The educational system in America enables a pathway to student success by connecting students to either college or career paths. In the marketplace, the business world provides training, mentorship, or internships to allow workers a pathway to success. However, in the church, there is a disconnect between student learning in Bible college or university and spiritual development in the spiritual marketplace of the local church. All the church had to do in the past was turn on their lights and unlock the doors, and people would come. That season in the church's life shifted, but many churches did not change with the times and held out hope that people would return.

Long before the pandemic, the church in North America was in a season of decline, and those numbers have accelerated since 2020. Still, instead of looking backward, the church can begin to look outward as they revamp how they reconnect with the community.

Church Connector

For many, the church has become fragmented through political polarization, social wedge issues, and cultural correctness that has forced Christians to pick sides, leaving a segment of the population disengaged during weekly services. The lack of connectedness has been pushed into the spotlight even more once the pandemic ended, as up to a quarter of members did not return to the local church. Instead of seeing the lack of a return as a negative, the church has a real opportunity to redouble its efforts to build a stronger core with which it can relaunch back into the community.

Reconnecting with current members will vary from church to church. Still, it will have a similar foundation built on personal relationships, one-on-one interactions outside of the church, small-group gatherings in homes or in the community doing life together, and serving in the church on teams. Each of these core components will help restore faith in the local church, reestablish camaraderie in each other, and strengthen the familial bond in partnership with the local church.

Neighborhood Connector

Decades before, church planters came to the neighborhood and planted a church, not to watch it die, but to grow over time. Where once neighbors walked to church, they now pass by, not thinking twice about the activities that are taking place inside the four walls. One must observe that if the neighborhood does not recognize that the church is alive, the church must begin to reengage and develop connections by going outside its walls.

With the challenges the church faces today, they can begin reimagining what the church would look like in the neighborhood for this season in which they find themselves—hosting annual block parties, opening up the parking lot for neighborhood garage sales, teaming up with a social service agency to host a bike rodeo where the church brings young families on the property to speak about bike safety, or hosting informal classes in partnership with an area vocational school or community college. Anything and everything that can show the church is alive is what needs to take place.

Community Connector

The church is called to "go," but for far too many, they are in a retreat position regarding community engagement and outreach. As the culture has shifted, the church has felt the hostile pushback from a society that has changed norms, and the church has struggled to adapt in love. While the Word of God will never change, how the Word is shared must adapt to the times. This is not new; in Jesus' time, he shared through his life and ministry that he was adaptable to the situation he found himself in over time. He was the same Jesus, teaching the same message, but did it in a way that spoke directly to His audience. As the church in the twenty-first century, so too must leaders today adapt to the audience they are speaking to but never water down the message.

In a day and age where mental health issues are on the rise, the church must become a safe place for individuals to walk through life with. Instead of challenging everything, why not show love? Instead of debating, why not listen? Instead of judging, why not extend grace? What an opportunity that the church has to live out the values and teachings of the Bible by being Jesus to those living in sin, struggling with addiction, or needing a word of encouragement.

Global Outreach Connector

Most denominations have a strong missional emphasis that calls the church outside of itself. But, when a church retreats, they tend to disconnect from outside ministry that does not directly impact the local church. A connector church serves locally and internationally to expand the gospel for Jesus. The missional arm of your denomination or network is a powerful resource to tap into and to sow through financial, spiritual, and relational giving. When a church is in crisis, there is a tendency to look inward when the Word of God is calling the church to look outward.

Connect with a missionary or global area and develop a long-term partnership where the missional heart around the world becomes a place for the mission of the church to be lived out daily through investments of prayer, giving, and service. There is a saying that we, the church, are "better together"; there is no doubt that when a church serves locally and globally, the church truly becomes the hands and feet of Jesus in action.

As the world changes around the church, be a church that finds innovative ways to reconnect with the outside by loving like Christ and living out the faith as a connector over the rough spiritual waters of the world.

GROWING RELATIONSHIPS RATHER THAN NUMBERS

In ministry, the word "church growth" has become the hallmark of the attractional model, which i That person determines their faith. nvests in experiences more than relationships over time. The established church has felt the residual effects of decades of trying to keep up with this attractional model. They have attempted to match the attractional model worship experiences and failed because they lacked the resources. Matching dollar for dollar or person to person will quickly outstrip the average size church of its resources. The pandemic exposed that beyond the bells and whistles of the high-gloss church is a lack of discipleship making and a focus on numbers rather than a life change.

When a church focuses on growing relationships rather than numbers, they begin to sense the heart of God in a new way. Experience has shown that investing in a person rather than a situation establishes a deeper, more meaningful connection than just a one-and-done event. The community outside your church's doors does not need another concert but a relationship with the Father that can change and transform their lives.

Focus on the Person, Not the Number They Represent

Any organization you belong to has metrics to track the progress the company or organization is making in the right direction. The church world is no different, yet the end of the quarter or yearly numbers do not always tell the true story of a life impacted through the ministry. While the church is a nonprofit business and can use principles found in the business world to help it sustain and grow its mission, it should not be arbitrarily focused on the bottom line and miss the God lines in between the balance sheets. The person who enters the local church or is reached by its members can be transformed into God's image and never tithe to the church. Should that person be less valued on the balance sheet because they cannot give back to the local church? Surely not.

When a church focuses on the person as a whole and not the transactional relationship, they see Christ in the person and not the person inside the local church, which begins to tear the veil of developing relationships to become pew warmers. Instead, the church sees a person as a life- change waiting to happen with God's help. The name of the person that has given their heart to Jesus then far outpaces a giving report and should be honored from a perspective that reminds the church of its true calling.

See the Value in the Person's Abilities Rather than the Church's Needs

I love the small church because I have pastored within her walls. I have served as the preacher, janitor, Sunday school teacher, and gardener. Coming from a "small church" mindset, I have experienced what many pastors experience week-in-week-out. Their value is found in the bulletin or number board near the front wall where they preach. The numbers were printed to remind the church of how many they had, and instead of providing value, they offered shame and personal embarrassment for the pastor.

As the established church rethinks its next steps, it must begin to see the value of each person rather than what the person's value can be for the church. While your local church might have tremendous needs, those needs cannot be whitewashed through a new tither or new body on the church council. Instead, it is through meaningful relationships that lives become impacted through relationships built over time outside the four walls of the church that begin to make a difference. Each person who comes across your path is a life that needs to be transformed or strengthened through a deeper relationship with Jesus. Jesus, through you, can impact the person in front of you. Valuing the person for who they are and not what they can do for the local church releases the pressure from winning them into membership and instead focuses on mentoring them into a deeper walk with Jesus.

Be a Difference-Maker in Their Life

The church is a small part of a person's larger life story. Yet, for most church members, it becomes the story in which they live their lives. While I love the local church, the church can keep you so busy doing church that you miss why you go in the first place. Stop momentarily and ask, *Who do I know that needs Jesus?* The person that is recalled by the Holy Spirit is the one in whose life you are called to make a difference. It is not by accident they came to mind. God needs you to see that you are the difference- maker in helping them connect with him and, as an extension, your local church.

So, what is the next step? Reach out, touch, and be Jesus. Reaching is pausing what you are doing and making a phone call, texting, or emailing the person. If you have time and are near the person, stop in and let them know you are thinking about them. As you move from reaching out, think about the next touch point, a connection where you can go deeper. Find a way to effectively communicate with the person by asking them about their needs and what is happening in their life. Stay focused more on them than you. The third step in being a difference maker is Jesus. Be there for them in the good and bad times as Jesus has been for your ministry. Encourage and lift them up by cheering them on when they need it. We have all been there, attending a church but feeling disconnected from the true church around us. Be Jesus, who loved the unlovable, cared about the sinner, and provided hope to the fallen.

I sense in my spirit that God is calling his church to grow deeper with people and to live life with them outside one hour a week on a Sunday morning. Let me challenge you to pray like never before that God would bring a person or people across your path to pour into so you can watch how God grows that relationship deeper and wider like never before.

Chapter 5

Discipleship
*Developing Christlike Followers
to Reach Outside*

When the church looks out from its protective cocoon and onto the world outside its property line, there is a tendency to fear the change around it. Over time, Christians have come face to face with challenging situations and have always overcome them. Today it is no different. The God of Abraham and Isaac is still the God of the church today. So why do we worry? Why do we want to give up when God calls us to share the good news with others?

From 1968–2001, Fred McFeely Rogers, better known to decades of children as Mr. Rogers, hosted a show that brought values of respect, community compassion, and love for neighbors to the forefront. During the ever-changing society when the show aired, the values found in Rogers's seminary training as a Presbyterian pastor were lived out in a safe place where a child's understanding could learn and grow. Those biblical values are equally needed today in a world that has edged closer to a secular society. In Luke 10:38–42, we meet two sisters (Martha and Mary) who open up their house to several traveling strangers, and amongst their leadership is Jesus. As Jesus comes in, Martha busily begins to prepare the home for a meal and turn down beds, but her sister Mary stops what she is doing, sits at her neighbors' feet, and listens to the stories told by the travelers.

At this moment, these sisters diverge and teach us a valuable lesson to reflect on.

Be Intentional about Your Responsiveness

Without a doubt Martha wanted to be a good host. Her actions belied that fact as she went about the house preparing for the company she welcomed into her home. In an instant, Martha did what many would do: she focused on the need, but interestingly, her sister, Mary, focused on the guests' wants. The household needed the guests to be fed and a place to sleep, while these travelers only desired to find a quick place to rest for the night out of the elements.

How often has your ministry focused on the need and missed the want? Countless times in my ministry, I have been so focused on doing that I missed the why behind it. I can see much of myself in Martha; maybe you can too. Martha missed the intentional meeting time with her guests because she was more focused on their needs than those in her living room. On the other hand, Mary knew the need; she probably heard the pots and pans banging around in the kitchen or even her sister mumbling under her breath about how she was not helping but entertaining the guests. Mary ignored the passions of her sister and provided her guests with a place to put up their feet, wash up from a long journey, and then sat at their feet.

Mary was intentional about responding to the wants of those she was engaging in. As a ministry leader, sometimes you must slow down to see where God is leading. Martha moved, and Mary sat. One missed Jesus, and one encountered Jesus. Let me challenge you to be intentional about your responsiveness and allow Jesus to guide your ministry.

Focus on Interactions, Not on Distractions

The sisters certainly knew of Jesus and his teachings. In a way, they must have been excited to have him and his followers in their home. There is a tendency to focus on the work of ministry week in and week out and miss the opportunity to experience ministry in your heart. Martha was a diligent, godly servant who had given all to serve the Lord. She was prepared to do it rather than be served herself. She could have found a respite and renewal but focused on ministry work instead. Some could say, bravo, she took the teachings and was living them out. But how many ministry leaders have fallen from grace because they were so busy serving that they became spiritually empty?

On the other hand, Mary focused on interactions at that moment and not the distractions from what needed to be done right then. She was present in the conversation and allowed the situation to unfold organically. She limited the distractions of her sister and focused on the one who came to visit. What an example of surrendering it all to be with Jesus. When you look at the worship folder each week, what do you see? Programs, interactions, and opportunities to serve? But, sometimes, the programs and interactions overwhelm the serving opportunities and become burdensome. The ministry burdened Martha, while Mary saw the chance to be with Jesus. So too, in your ministry, you can be so focused on serving that you miss the interactions God has placed right in front of you.

Refrain from allowing the distractions of ministry to overwhelm your sense of servanthood by sometimes being served by others. Allow God to speak to you by pausing, waiting, praying, and listening to what God has for you. Your ministry will be better for it.

Build Interpersonal Relationships with Others Outside of Church

There is a tendency in the church to focus on what is before you. The worship folder that needs folding, the bathrooms that need cleaning, or the class that requires a teacher, and you miss the relationships that are waiting to be connected because you get trapped into the cycle of doing, and not the process of seeing. Martha was so trapped in doing the work that she missed seeing Jesus' right before her. She is not alone. If you are the average church leader, you have felt that cycle and can look back and see where you were so busy that you missed your blessing.

I am more convinced than ever that the church's work is outside than inside of it. The world is steadily going to hell, and the church is not even pulling the fire alarm to let the world know there is a fire. We must do a better job. Mary not only heard but saw the teachings of Jesus up close and personal, and she was determined to focus on the relationship rather than the results of her sister huffing and puffing around the house. She identified not with her sister at that moment but with Jesus. She sought his interest, listened to his stories, and sought to communicate with him through sitting rather than doing.

As a leader, you must permit yourself to leave your office to build relationships. Allow time in your weekly schedule to interact and learn from others. If you serve bivocationally, find ways to develop relationships with non-church friends. Be a Mary in their lives. Sit down and listen to their life story, and then share how Jesus has helped you.

Sally Susman, the Chief Corporate Affairs Officer of Pfizer, said in a post on the blog *Thrive Global*, "A pause is not a period. It's a comma. A breath. A moment filled with so much opportunity to make the right decision."[1] If we can learn anything from the story of these two sisters, it is to pause and reflect on how one can

---

1. Sally Susman, "How I Learned about the Power of Pause," *Thrive Global* (blog), March 28, 2023 (para. 7), https://community.thriveglobal.com/how-i-learned-about-the-power-of-pause/.

do ministry better. Sometimes, you become busy doing church, but you should not stay so busy that you miss Jesus. Focus on what is happening before you, and take advantage of the lessons being taught and learn from them.

If you are in a Martha situation right now, there is still time to evaluate and move towards a Mary posture of sitting at Jesus' feet. The good thing is Jesus is still in the house if you will take notice.

BECOMING A HOUSE OF PRAYER

Most small church leaders realize that when the time comes to address the needs of potential guests, those who have remained for years begin to push back on the notion that new people need to be brought in to help the church. New blood sometimes brings out bad blood for those who held onto power as the church decreased in attendance. The story of Martha and Mary shows the parallel lives and cost of not paying attention to the guests who visit the church. Jesus, throughout his ministry, showed a remarkable tact of decentralizing the mission by empowering his disciples while at the same time handing off responsibility to those around him. This two-for-one approach allowed the disciples to carry forth the ministry of Jesus long after he ascended into heaven. Being taught and empowered to serve the disciples brought the teaching of Christ beyond the 200-mile radius that Jesus ministered in and has touched the lives of billions throughout the centuries.

The church (your church) must have a missional plan to connect with guests other than a gift bag and connection card when a guest walks through the church's front doors. The missional strategy is not a secret plan or strategy given to large churches, but a simple plan found within Christ's teachings. Jesus taught that his followers needed to gather and go.

Gather to Pray

If you serve in the average church, your services are most likely scripted down to how long it will take you or someone else to pray. How the North American church got into such a mess, I do not know. I know that it is not unique to your church or even mine. It's become a phenomenon that has put the Holy Spirit in a box so that the people could be in and out within one hour. One of the most potent words given in the Bible is found in the books of Matthew and Mark when Jesus says (Mark 11:17 NIV) he writes, and as he taught them, he said, "Is it not written: 'My house will be called a house of prayer for all nations'? How can your local church be a House of Prayer if the house is locked to the will of God? My friend, you are not alone. Tens of thousands of churches want to be God-centered places of worship but turn into man-centered worship centers that rely on their power and only call on God when trouble strikes. Reporter Ryan Foley, writing for the *Christian Post*, cites a poll conducted with Braun Research of one thousand respondents surveyed in April of 2020 that only "45% of adults surveyed claimed that they pray every day." And of that, "65% of adults said that they prayed at least once a week, but not daily."[2] The poll was at the beginning of an unfolding global pandemic that would ultimately take over 1.1 million Americans' lives.[3] If the church would not stop and pray during a 100-year global pandemic, how can the church expect to become an authentic house of prayer today?

Prayer Meetings Change Things

Have you ever called a prayer meeting at the church? How many showed up? If you have been to the ones I attended, it's typically

---

2. Ryan Foley, "Only 45% of Americans Say They Pray on a Daily Basis, Survey Finds," *Christian Post*, October 8, 2020 (paras. 4–5), https://www.christianpost.com/news/only-45-of-americans-say-they-pray-on-a-daily-basis-survey.html

3. "US COVID-19 Cases and Deaths by State," https://usafacts.org/visualizations/coronavirus-covid-19-spread-map

less than ten people. I used to get so discouraged by the low attendance number, but today, I celebrate that ten people chose to pause, pray, and participate in a prayer meeting recently held. According to the research poll cited earlier, "Just 15% of those surveyed said they never prayed, while the remaining 17% said that they pray irregularly."[4] So, it makes sense that only a handful show up and pray when church leaders call a prayer meeting. Some time ago, God placed in my heart to call my local church to prayer. Why? Because we had many needs that needed addressing, at the very least, no visitors or at least none that would stay. Each Wednesday from 10 am–12 pm, the church is called to prayer. Within the first three weeks of the focused prayer time, God provided two major blessings as we began to turn his House into a House of Prayer. A church member donated $50,000 to help with our physical needs, as we are a legacy church with a lot of deferred maintenance that we have begun to address. Within hours of that donation, the church received word that a former member had passed away and left a quarter of a million-dollar estate to the church to go towards our homeless ministry program.

Celebrate What Happens through Prayer

Some may say, well, that was luck or just timing, and I say, look at God! When the church humbled themselves in prayer, God began to move on our behalf. Please do not hear what I am not saying. If you pray, riches will not be dropped in your lap. But, when you pray, God begins to move on your behalf like never before, opening the church up for a future God move. When focused and deliberate, prayer can restore what the enemy has stolen. It can heal wounds caused by church strife and change the outlook of even the most hardened heart. Let me encourage you to find ways to keep prayer at the center of the church. It is good to pray alone in your prayer closet, but something begins to happen when God's people gather and pray for the church's needs. Whatever the need,

---

4. Foley, "Only 45% of Americans," para. 7.

wherever you gather as a church, begin to lift the needs in prayer and do it together. Trust me, I have witnessed it; God moves when the church begins to pray. What do you have to lose? Try it. Call your local church to pray weekly for an extended period. If only two or three show up, celebrate. Suppose fifty people participate, then celebrate. Allow the Spirit of God to dictate the time and spiritual effort put forth. Trust the God process as you gather and turn his House into a House of Prayer.

PREPARING TO GO SHARE JESUS

Why is sharing Jesus with others so hard? It seems simple at the outset, but sharing their faith with a stranger is scary for many Christians. Church members have learned that discipleship-making is not for the spiritual faint of heart. It is spiritual work because you must be proactive and not reactive to the environment around you. You must be open to the Holy Spirit's prompting and rely on God's power, not your own. Even Jesus was challenged for his faith and beliefs but was willing to keep sharing and listening even to the naysayers. If guests were to come to your local church and stay, what would you do with them? If there is no discipling mechanism, they will slip back out the same door they entered. So, before you move from the pew to the street to share the gospel, know why you are going out to share the gospel. Before you ask someone to come to the church, understand why they should go and stay as a member of your local church.

Prepare Your Own Heart

In Luke 10:25–37, Jesus shares the parable of the Good Samaritan as he was confronted about his teachings by an expert in the law. Much like in the world today, Jesus was questioned, as the expert in the law wanted to trap Jesus. Somebody might even question your faith and why you believe, and if you are not ready to respond, you will fall flat on your spiritual face. Prepare your heart by preparing your mind, body, and soul. Read the Word, remember the Word, recite the Word, and live out the Word. Jesus did not stumble when questioned; he shared a story of three examples of being a neighbor. Like Jesus, be ready to share your faith journey and how God has transformed your life.

As Jesus shared the parable, the one he spoke to was looking for a reason to catch him in a mistake rather than learn from him, but that did not stop Jesus from sharing. You might even be faced with backlash for sharing your faith or receive a discouraging word, but stay focused on the reason you did it in the first place: to share Jesus with the world.

Partner with God to See What He Sees

The story of the Samaritan spurred and even provoked the expert of the law because the Samaritan would not have been a faithful Jew in his eyes because of the mixed-race heritage of the Samaritan. However, Jesus used the example because he was partnering with God to share Old Testament truths through a New Testament revelation that pushed back on the idea that God was for only one race and not all. The person with whom you share the good news of Jesus might have been hurt in the past by another Christian, a church, or society quoting Scripture. Be gentle, be understanding, and recognize that what a person says back to your invitation to God is a response to their hurts and desires, not God's. Do not take one adverse reaction to mean to stop sharing your faith. Instead, partner with God to see what he sees in the person you share your faith with.

Those who heard Jesus that day responded to the confrontation and learned valuable lessons that will be lesson markers for you today:

1. Not everyone will be receptive to the message of the cross.
2. A person determines their faith.
3. If a heart is open, God will change his/her life.

4. If a heart is closed, it remains closed to the invitation of God.
5. What you share is as important as what is received by the person you are sharing with.

Participate in Long-Term Discipleship-Making

Maybe you came to Christ as a young child. For me, I was twenty-two years old. What if someone who shared Christ with me gave up because they thought I was too old? How many people have missed Jesus because someone did not stop and share the gospel? The one who was beaten and left for dead in the parable Jesus shared missed being helped by two others (a priest and a Levite) before the Samaritan helped the man. Ask yourself, *Am I a priest, Levite, or a Samaritan?* God brings across your path daily individuals who need you to support, encourage, and love like Jesus. Yet, by the wayside are the discarded castaways, taken in by the world, not the church.

The law expert needed to have the compassion that Jesus showed and missed the proper understanding of Jesus' teaching. Jesus, on the other hand, left there and began a continued journey to share the gospel, teach his disciples about living out the law, connecting Scripture to modern-day issues, and staying faithful to God as a living example of holiness. While the expert missed out, the disciples followed Jesus, spending years with him learning at his feet. What you do today matters more tomorrow than today. When you invest, spend time, and walk with a person learning about faith, you become the Samaritan who provides long-term care for the injured.

Jesus taught that you could stay in the temple and have a lot of head knowledge and miss the reason you learned what you have learned, or you could go outside the temple walls and live out the knowledge by sharing Jesus with the lost and hurting.

Chapter 6

The Community in Crises
Be Jesus in the Face of Trouble

THERE HAS BEEN AN ebb and flow of church growth throughout human history. Oppression from governments, people groups, or institutions have tried to keep the Christian faith in a downward spiral. But repeatedly, God has used the negative and turned it in his favor. Think about it this way: where a small group gathers to worship him, he uses that tiny ember to light a spiritual spark that has grown to over "2.6 billion Christians" in 2023.[1] While spiritual headwinds have faced the church in North America, God's word is still transforming people's spiritual hearts and minds worldwide. Lifeway Research reported, "almost 7 in 10 U.S. Protestant pastors (69%) believe there is a growing sense of fear within their congregations about the future of the nation and world. Additionally, more than 3 in 5 (63%) say their churches have a similar increasing dread specifically about the future of Christianity in the U.S. and around the world."[2] With the church struck by the mental double

---

1. "Status of Global Christianity 2024," https://www.gordonconwell.edu/center-for-global-christianity/resources/status-of-global-christianity/.

2. Aaron Earls, "Fear Prevalent in Pews, according to Protestant Pastors," *Outreach Magazine*, August 23, 2023 (para. 2), https://outreachmagazine.com/

whammy of pastors and churchgoers fearing the loss of their Christian faith and the downturn in the spiritual and economic economy of the church's life, how can they be moved to win the lost for Christ while in their spiritual crises?

Each week, pastors stand in the pulpit and look out on half-empty sanctuaries, preaching the Word with power and conviction, but fewer and fewer people are hearing the message of the good news. While pastors and lay leaders fear the future, they must begin to recognize that with God, they can overcome any challenge and obstacle that is before them. It starts by seeing Jesus in those around them. The parking lot may be half-full each Sunday, but the big-box-store lots are filled with people seeking enjoyment. Realize there is not a lack of people but a lack of sowing into the gospel field as a missionary for Christ. "Only 3 in 10 unchurched Americans (29%) say a Christian has ever shared with them one-on-one how a person becomes a Christian, according to Lifeway Research."[3] The community is in crisis because the church does not rely on Christ as its guide.

Do Ministry That Matters

Every community has a section of town that people try to avoid. Why? Because it is dangerous. But what about the people that must live there? Don't they need a church that rises over fear and into faith? One Sunday morning, I pulled into the church parking lot to the shouts of several homeless individuals yelling at each other. The church has a compassionate ministry called His Mission, which has been around for nearly three decades and feeds, clothes, and helps those who need an extra hand. Within minutes, two cop cars pulled up, and the people experiencing homelessness began scattering. Later, I found out a few new guests felt disrespected by

---

resources/77221-fear-prevalent-in-pews-according-to-protestant-pastors.html

3. Aaron Earls, "22 Vital Stats for Ministry in 2022," *Lifeway Research*, January 5, 2022 (para. 13), https://research.lifeway.com/2022/01/05/22-vital-stats-for-ministry-in-2022/.

another couple, and a verbal brawl spilled out of the gym and into the parking lot. Some would say the ministry was too dangerous to continue, but we see the need and want to be the hands and feet of Jesus.

I must be frank with you; I am tired of doing "ministry safe." Ministry safe has slowly killed the Christian church because bottoms in the seats and weekly offerings became more important than lives transformed with the gospel. Jesus did not die on the cross for big buildings or more cars in the parking lot but for those stuck in sin. You might have heard that when Rome burned, Nero played the fiddle. The dichotomy of the matter is that the church is allowing surrounding communities to burn all around them, while they sit in their comfortable empty building, watching and waiting for Christ's return. While it cannot be verified whether or not Nero actually played the fiddle as Rome fell to shambles around him, the same cannot be said about most local churches—we can see it happening before our eyes.

Outside the church's doors, there is a ministry. The church must be willing to get uncomfortable to serve in difficult areas and to seek the need to see the transformation take place not only in those they are helping but in their own lives.

Invest Resources Where It Can Help

I have never been at a church where I have not heard, "Where will we get the money for that?" One church I served had over $350,000 in the bank and no debt, yet I still heard those words. Sure, churches must live within their means; however, they should never seek to lower their ministry viewpoint to the budget number on the page. Why have faith if the numbers mark it dead? "2022 marks the first time since 2016 that more than half of pastors feel the economy is having a negative impact on their churches and the first time since 2012 that fewer than 10% of pastors see the economy as having a positive effect."[4] Yet, statistics go on to say

---

4. Aaron Earls, "Half of Pastors Say the Economy Is Hurting Their Church," *Lifeway Research*, October 11, 2022. https://

that most churches have seen that giving has increased. "Around 7 in 10 U.S. Protestant pastors say giving at their church so far this year is at or exceeding their budget, including 46% who say giving has been about what was budgeted and 23% who say it's higher. Close to 3 in 10 (29%) say giving is below their 2022 budget."[5] So, what is happening? The wrong resource is being shared. The mind has overcame the heart. God did not call his people to hide, but live out their faith, faithfully.

Where in your community today needs a gospel witness? What partnership can be forged to secure a God advancement? There are people, places, and partnerships willing for you and your church to walk alongside them. What will it take for your local church to become a church on a mission? Whatever resources the local church has left (people, property, or finances), leverage them to expand and equip the kingdom of God.

Change the Spiritual Scorecard

The way the world measures effectiveness must not be the same way the church does. The scorecard that the church has used for decades has become broken. Measuring effectiveness by buildings, programs, and money is a surefire way to deflate the kingdom of God down to numbers and miss the souls impacted by the gospel. When you have read the Bible, what scorecard did Jesus' use?

1. Life change happens through seeking forgiveness.
2. Returning what was taken through sin and restoring what was lost through Christ's blood.
3. People matter more than their position in the world.
4. Love overcomes all sin when the sinner repents of their sin.

Begin to see the world outside of the church as a place Jesus is calling. Adapt to the needs around you and not the conditions

research.lifeway.com/2022/10/11/half-of-pastors-say-the-economy-is-hurting-their-church/.
  5. Earls, "Half of Pastors," para. 7.

inside of you. Capture the Christ spirit you have learned about inside the church and begin to spread it wherever you go daily. The community around you needs the message of God's saving grace, but who will tell them if not you? The scorecard of the ministry is changing. It is no longer "bigger is better," but people over things, love over hate, forgiveness over condemnation. Be Jesus in the face of trouble, and watch how God uses you and your church to transform lives and the community in which you live.

BUILDING A COMPASSIONATE COMMUNITY

The story of the small church is not unique to size or community. The struggles that your local church has gone through in the last few years is a story played out in communities near and far from your own. When trouble comes to the local church, there is a tendency to feel isolated and ashamed that your leadership is faltering, and the church is declining. Still, that retreat posture only positions the church's leadership to make decisions that will ultimately harm, not help, the local community or the church.

As you look out on the landscape of your community from the perspective of your small church perch, you might have asked what can we do to help the community? The one thing a faltering church typically has is space. Empty classrooms, parking lots, education buildings, or offices. How can your local church leverage vacant areas to help the community? It takes a reimagining of what was to see what could be. The process is easy for outsiders but very difficult for those who have been a part of the church for an extended period. Spend some time walking around the church campus. Write down where you observe extra space that can be leveraged for one to two hours a week to be used more often by the community.

How Can the Church Serve Locally

Every community has needs. What those needs are and how other churches or nonprofits are meeting them can only be answered through an honest analysis of the local community you serve. There are opportunities outside the church's doors if you brainstorm the need; who in the community is meeting the demand for services, what conditions need to be met in the marketplace, etc. An idea sparked inside the brainstorming session with your leadership team (church board, church council, deacons, elders, or influential members) will bear fruit in the future. Once the church defines the need that is not met within the care continuum within the community, reflect on how your local church can fill the gap or host a nonprofit agency on your site.

While some may look at all the steeples in town and ask why we would need another church ministry, know that the spiritual marketplace is not saturated, and that God wants to use your church to focus on living out your Christian faith beyond a Sunday morning service. The church of Christ should not just be a building used once a week but a place where life is lived out seven days a week on and off campus, serving a higher calling. What an opportunity to turn space that is no longer in use at the church and put it to use for new kingdom opportunities. If you are creative and open, God will take a dream and turn it into reality.

What Resources Can the Church Leverage to Help the Community

As the church leadership brainstormed and evaluated the property's current and future uses, begin to see what God could do if the church were open to serving in a new way. If repurposed, the empty classroom or classroom filled with forgotten stuff from the past could be used to do something new. I get it; change is never easy, but this type of change can transform loss into gain. Think about it this way: When partnering with a for-profit or nonprofit organization, your local church can redeem a space waiting for use. While you might think you need more money, God sees the people helped through a new partnership. Isaiah 43:19 says, 'See, I am doing a new thing! Now it springs up; do you not perceive it? I am making a way in the wilderness and streams in the wasteland.' Many small churches focus on people, money, and time to either expand or cut community outreach when the budget is reviewed. What about focusing on God? God is calling your local church out of the wilderness of decline by using a perceived weakness (empty classrooms or space) and using it to expand your ministry footprint by partnering with other agencies within the community to provide services.

Let me challenge you to be willing to allow God to lead. Here is an example: At my current assignment, decades ago, the church had on average 600 people, hosted a K-12 Christian school, and was filled weekly with activities. Today, she runs much lower than that, with no school and empty buildings. While we could blame twenty-five years of decline on various situations or leaders, the church has redirected its outlook on creatively reusing God's property. The former school is rented to a private daycare. Two empty buildings on the property now form the basis of a new thrift store, food pantry, homeless ministry, and future compassionate ministry center. The gymnasium, used primarily for eight weeks a year for upward basketball, has now become a community center used in partnership with the Boys & Girls Club, a walking club, children's church, and a host of community sporting events. So, what changed? Our outlook. We took a perceived negative and have turned it to God's advantage. Even the 1,200-person seat sanctuary has had thirty pews removed. With future designs for expanded coffee and gathering areas added there instead.

This is an example of the people surrendering and God moving on our behalf. Do not overcomplicate things by saying what you do not have. Begin by seeing what you do have to offer God and trust him. When you do, you begin to take a negative and turn it into a positive, which leads to a compassionate community of believers.

INVITING THE COMMUNITY ONTO THE CAMPUS

The church board has invited the community to share space in a future partnership. Now what? Let me provide a note of caution: There will be a tendency to begin declaring lines in the sand between current members and partners renting, leasing, or sharing space inside the church facility. Maybe not by you, but trust me, by church leaders, elected and unelected, who will say they have the church's best interest at heart. The truth is that change is hard, and some folks will react the opposite way you would expect them to act. Church leadership might cite legal responsibility to slow down the process of uniting in a shared space or begin to bicker over a room not picked up or a light left on. In the grander scheme of things, these small, mundane things can consume the positive momentum of the partnership and turn it into a dreadful one. As a church leader, you must help guard against the tendency of others to unwind forward progress.

Your voice as a church leader can help extinguish a harmful fire of words and actions or fan the flames that could destroy the partnership. Your position within the church has been entrusted to you by God and should be taken hold of by such. Help lead your leadership team and church to see the possible opportunities, and when an issue arises, help them navigate it with God's grace.

Embrace the Change the Community Has Brought

Sharing space where once it had been empty is an exciting prospect for a church that has been in steady decline. Once classrooms were filled with church families; today, through local partnerships, they are turned into offices for nonprofits, childcare classrooms for a for-profit business, or space for future rental income through parties, meeting space, or hosting a homeschool co-op. There are endless opportunities to turn unused space into community space, but it will take a flexible and agile leadership eye to embrace change.

It will be easy to see any negative that comes forth, such as an overflowing trash can or chipped paint on a hallway door. But focus on the God-moments of individuals coming to the church seeking help, families feeling safe dropping off their children or just more cars in the parking lot. As a leader, if you embrace the change in the community, you will see the hand of God all over it. Subsequently, if you look hard enough, you will see harmful components that can destroy the God partnership that is before you. Let me remind you that your local church, possibly even you, prayed for more people to come to the church. While they might not come on Sunday, God used the prayers, property, and space to fill them with community members and to bless the local church.

Encourage Fostering Deeper Relationships

The church wants to grow and rebound from decline. They have taken the steps, reinvented space for potential use for new ministry opportunities, and cleaned the facility to prepare for future guests, and have now begun new partnerships. The mission field that seemed so far away has now entered the four walls of the church. What a God opportunity! What a chance to use your missionary skills to reach a potential new convert to Christ or even the local church. Find ways at least once a month where the church can pour out its love upon others. See these touchpoints as love points from God. Allow the church's hospitality to extend into the lives of these community members who share the space with church members.

Here are several ways to connect with this new community:

1. Provide breakfast to the community partners. Set up a breakfast station in the fellowship hall or lobby where these new rental partners can stop by throughout the morning and pick up a meal the church provides. The meal can be a formal breakfast or grab-and-go breakfast items. The idea is to let the partner know the church values the partnership.
2. Donate drinks and snacks, setting up a formal break room where employees or guests of the partnership can be provided with complimentary refreshments. On each refreshment,

stick a label with a Scripture verse and position a small sign near the items that let the partners know your church thanks them for their partnership.

3. Have the partner agency share during a church service what they are doing, and ask beforehand if there are any needs. During the service, share that need with the church and either collect items in the coming week to meet the need or take up a special offering. Either way, the focus is for the local church to see the partnership opportunities before them.

Be creative and allow your local context to dictate the response to this new partnership. However you choose to respond, serve like Jesus, act with compassion, and be charitable in your discourse.

Chapter 7

Close the Back Door
Keeping Guests You Have Won

I DID NOT GROW up on a farm but have spent many years pastoring in rural communities. I have seen large barns where owners keep their livestock, supplies, and tools for the homestead. It reminds me of a saying: "It is too late to close the barn door after the horse has left it." The saying means you cannot change something that has already happened. Is your local church trying to shut the barn door after the fact? If that is the case, you are not alone. Churches are bleeding members and new converts to the faith. Legacy churches have struggled to adapt to the ever-changing culture of their community. Churches have tried gimmicks, one-and-done outreach events that have hyped the church but become deflated because there lacks a successful follow-up model. The small church is forcing the door to close instead of trying new ways to keep the doors open. However, instead of fretting over the negative, see the challenge as an opportunity to learn from past mistakes, to reengage ministry in a new way, and to capture the moment by being community focused.

There is an aspect of the church that frustrates many church leaders. As a leader, you have prayed for the service, prepared for the service, arranged the service, arrived, and received your first of several complaints about issues, all before the church service even starts. Welcome to Sunday morning! It is a time when the Lord is to be honored, but more times than not, the devil is elevated through negative issues brought to the forefront. I am convinced that the evil one has the church so distracted by the mundane to keep it from focusing on the God-things before it. What would happen if the church prayed, sought new relationships as Christ sought one with you, or even entered the space open to allow the Spirit to move? The sinful nature cannot hinder the church, but a church where sin is called out, forgiven, removed, and relationships renewed in serving Christ above all weekly.

According to Marissa Postell Sullivan, "Pastors at the smallest churches, those fewer than 50 attendees, are the most likely to say less than 25% of their attendees are involved in a small group (39%)."[1] The smallest churches struggle to retain members, capture guests, retain guests, and support current members through a discipleship journey. In that case, the church is on a trajectory of closure rather than more exposure to the broader community. To increase the chances of guests being retained and becoming future members, I have developed a simple **Step 3 Initiative (Step In, Step Up, and Step Out)** to help you and your church leadership rethink how to retain guests.

STEP 3 INITIATIVE

The fact is that small churches think that because of their size, they can better connect with newcomers. But, have you ever had a friend visit your church as a secret guest-shopper and heard their response? Have you ever asked why the friendliest church in

---

1. Marissa Postell Sullivan, "Research Reveals Importance of Small Groups, Evangelism, Assimilation for Church Growth," *Lifeway Research*, March 7, 2023 (para. 6), https://research.lifeway.com/2023/03/07/research-reveals-importance-of-small-groups-evangelism-assimilation-for-church-growth/.

town cannot keep the average guest! Thom Rainer wrote, "Many leaders and members think their churches have better ministries than they really do. And many leaders think their churches are friendlier than they really are."[2] All churches, including mine, can do a better job with guest assimilation.

STEP IN

(GREET—GATHER—GLEAN)

Greet

If your church is like the average church, you try your best most Sundays to have a friendly greeter welcoming new- and- old comers with a warm smile, a friendly handshake, and providing the person with a worship bulletin. How you greet and who you greet is as vital as the sermon message. In today's digital age, guests check out the church online long before they attend. With that in mind, the message from the pulpit to the front door must be consistent. Developing a greeting team that is genuinely focused on the guest experience is essential. Ensure the team understands the value of seeing each person, not just those they know, as valuable to what could happen next. Long before the pastor shares the message or a song is sung, that interaction could either make or break a guest choosing to return or not.

Gather

Before the service, make sure the guest knows what to expect. If they are alone, ask if they would like to sit with one of the greeting team members. It could help them feel more at ease. By extending the traditional greeting from the door to the pew, you tell the guests that they matter. Before the service, explain what typically happens during service and highlight some points of interest in the worship bulletin that they might enjoy. The greeters should

---

2. Thom S. Rainer, *Becoming a Welcoming Church* (Nashville: B&H, 2010), 3.

focus not on the troubles the church might be having or what a week it has been for them but focus strictly on the guests, ensuring they feel welcomed, and their voice is heard by answering any questions they might have. There is a temptation to say too much or too little, so make sure the team is prayed up and allows the Holy Spirit to guide.

Glean

How often has a guest left, and the church has not received one piece of information from them? Too many times. As the guest waits for the service to start, share a "connection card" or informational card and have them fill it out. The greeting team should ensure that connection cards are put in the pew back with a working pen nearby to make it seamless enough for the visitor to fill out long before the service starts. When the offering plate is passed or if there is a welcome area, point out to the visitor where they should drop the card or take it to the welcome area for a special gift. If your church collects contact information, make sure your church does something about it. The office should follow up with a card, email, call, or text in the coming week.

STEP UP

(FOLLOW UP—FELLOWSHIP—FAMILY)

Follow Up

After the visitor has enjoyed the service and left their contact information, now what? How will the greeting team follow up with the visitor? Will there be a personal visit to the home, a letter from the pastor, or a gift card sent through a text? Whatever the church does, ensure it honors the person and God. I cannot tell you how many times I have witnessed information cards lie dormant on an office desk or thrown in the trash, unused. What that says to the guests when they are not contacted is that they were not valued.

Be a church that values guests by following up. In a world that is disconnected in so many ways. Be the church that intentionally connects through some means. I will allow you to figure out what works best in your local context, but let me stress: do something. Anything is better than ignoring the information card that has been filled out.

Fellowship

Before the guest leaves the service, ask them if they have any lunch plans. If they do not, invite them to a restaurant and share a meal with them and others from the church. During the meal, spend time listening, interacting, and not leaving them alone as there will be a tendency to focus on your friends. As you end the meal, do two things: invite the person back to church next Sunday and pick up the check. Even if they insist on picking up the tab, explain to them what a blessing it has been for you to visit with them, and picking up the check blesses your spirit to do so. Don't allow them to steal your blessing, and remember being a blessing is part of the fellowship of your church.

Family

As the next week approaches, reach out to your guest through an email, text message, or a phone call. Whatever communication tool works best in your local context should be followed. Following up on your fellowship by inviting them into the family (the local church) is important. How? Ask them to join you at Sunday school or a life group midweek. "Small groups and Sunday school classes provide the relational glue that allows a local congregation to be a place where people love one another. . . . Churches with few people participating in groups are not in a healthy position to be making more disciples," said Scott McConnell, executive director of Lifeway Research.[3] Small groups, by whatever name you call

---

3. Sullivan, "Research Reveals Importance," para. 5.

them, are the "glue" that can help meld old and new people in the church together. As the church grows through new families coming, these smaller groups create intimate spaces for people to live life together outside of the one-hour morning worship service.

STEP OUT

(PARTICIPATE—PARTNER—PROCESS)

Participate

As guests begin to attend more regularly, what will be the church's next steps to help them fully participate in the activities of the church? The goal should be to help them move from a guest to a member. Before they become a full-fledged member, the stopover area is to attend regularly by actively participating in classes and other activities that the church offers. There are times when guests begin coming for a few weeks or months, and suddenly, they stop attending or returning communications from the church. Most likely, it was not one thing that made them disconnect but a series of items. If a guest actively participates in a small group or other church activities, they are less likely to fall between the cracks. Relationships and connections are essential to sustaining a guest long-term. So be the church that ensures everyone is not only welcomed but encouraged to participate in the church's life.

Partner

The happiest people in the church are the ones who are on fire for the Lord. Those happy warriors are the ones who can influence and encourage people, so why not place them front and center? Traditionally, these people are new to the church or the Lord, who have not been corrupted by cliquish groups' negative words, and who sees the church positively. If you want to move your church from stagnant to growing again, you must win and keep new people. How? By sending the converts from your church back into the public square or marketplace. They will happily discuss Jesus and what your church has done for them. But sadly, many churches muzzle these excited people because they are not in leadership or have not gained access to the right people. Sometimes, the church must get out of the way and partner with people who love the Lord and will tell everyone about it.

Process

The guest becomes increasingly familiar with the church, and it is time to move them from the guest seat into the membership chair. Membership is not about the rules of a denomination or fellowship but about the heart of the person willing to join the church to reach more people for Jesus. If a first-time guest grows to love the church over the ensuing weeks and months, they will want to become a member. But it takes intentionality by the greeters, members, and pastor the first time they arrive. If the church is unable or willing to process the steps to get ready for a guest, to care for a guest, they will never get to the point where the guest becomes a member. Dr. Stan Toler and Alan Nelson wrote in their book *The Five Star Church*, "The Bible says that all Christians are to act as ambassadors, as liaisons between God and others. When we do things that reflect a shabby mind-set, we are certainly not representing Him well, because God does things with excellence."[4]

The process is more than going through the motions. The process is developing a team of passionate Jesus-followers willing to honor God by honoring guests while developing long-term relationships that help the guests move into membership. In chapter 2, I wrote about following up with first-time guests, but I want to reiterate to you that everything matters to the guests and should matter to the church.

---

4. Stan Toler and Alan Nelson, *The Five Star Church: Serving God and His People with Excellence* (Ventura, CA: Regal, 1999), 12.

7 WAYS TO GATHER VISITOR INFORMATION

In a world interconnected through technology, personal relationships seem disconnected due to the inability to have one-on-one conversations with other people. Before a guest enters the church, the church should think of ways to connect with them beyond a one-time visit to a service. If your church is to grow, it must be willing to meet new converts to the faith in a way that provides community rather than just connection. Here are seven clear ways to engage visitors.

1. **Share in a conversation:** Sounds simple, yet you would be surprised how many visitors are never spoken to or engaged besides, "welcome," or "thanks for coming!" Before handing a guests a connection or information card, try to develop a commonality before you ask for private information. If guests choose not to share their information with the church, respect their privacy and be friendly. It may take two or three visits before they feel comfortable sharing their data; that is okay and should be respected. The key is not gathering information but developing a relationship through personal interaction each time you see them. One of the ways to connect is to remember names or at least the name of a child. Small connections can make a big difference.

2. **Connect personally:** Everyone on the welcome team should be trained to greet and guide guests from the time they walk into the building until they leave. Instead of just gathering information, focus on connecting personally with the person or family. Before they leave, make sure a person on the welcome team introduces them to the pastor or at least alerts the pastor that a new family is here and points them out so the pastor can connect. Through a pastoral conversation, the pastor might want to invite them to coffee or a meal on the church to connect more personally after church or in the week ahead.

3. **Passive Connections:** QR Codes are an easy way to gather information from guests that attend a service. Place these codes in and around the facility for guests to connect on their own time. Codes can be placed on the back of a pew directly in front of where someone sits, inserted into the bulletin, at the children's check-in, or even on the bathroom mirror. The goal is to provide multiple avenues for guests to connect and not to feel pressured to be acknowledged by the church by being handed a card, asked to wear a guest badge, or standing up during the service to be recognized. Passive connections enable the guests to engage in their own way and time.

4. **Keep the Connection Card Simple:** How much information will the church use? Ponder that question before developing a connection card that gathers information from a first-time guest. Many preprinted information cards ask for too much irrelevant information that the church does not need. In today's world, people want to keep information private. Instead of asking for too much information, keep it simple: name (first and last), email address, personal address, or phone number to contact them. Let the guest choose one or all three after sharing their first and last name with the church.

5. **Honor the Guest for Attending:** Today's guest wants to be a part of something, not just experience it as an outsider. Invite guests to fill out the connection card, and in return, the local church will donate funds in honor of the guest to a local missional outpost of their choice. Add to the bottom of the connection card several missional outposts the church invests in and encourage the guest to circle one of the choices. Circling a missional outreach allows them to partner with the church but also reinforces that the church cares about people and programs outside the four walls of the campus.

6. **Provide a Gift:** If you honor a guest with a gift, make sure it is tied directly back to the church's mission and not just a gift for attending. If you give away a coffee mug, pen, or T-shirt, make sure it has the church's logo, mission, and

other pertinent information as a reminder to the guest of the church and its mission. A creative way to engage guests is to host a monthly drawing where you collect all connection cards and draw out a card to award a more significant gift to that person or family. The drawing is a way to reconnect with a guest who may not have come since the first visit. Or provide an opportunity once a month to meet with the pastor over pizza (Pizza with a Pastor) as a way to have any guest questions answered directly from the pastor.

7. **Follow-Up:** Whatever you do as a church, plan a follow-up strategy to reach out to a first-time guest. That can entail sending a letter from the pastor, emailing, or mailing a gift card from a local coffee shop on behalf of the church, calling or texting an invite back to church, or a personal visit from church members. Whatever your local church chooses to do, plan on doing something. If a guest fills out a guest's card, the church should acknowledge that in some tangible way.

While this is not an exhaustive list, hopefully, one or all of these ways of gathering guests' information will stimulate your welcome team to discuss ways to engage first-time guests. At the end of the day, if your church wants to keep guests, you must first be ready for guests. Close the church's back door by being ready at the front door!

Chapter 8

Developing Guests into Future Leaders

As the church begins to win new visitors, invariably, there will be pushback from current members who feel threatened by the "invasion" of new people, thoughts, and actions. As a church leader, you must find new ways to integrate the old and the new into church membership. Threading the needle without alienating the old and recent converts will need to be done through prayer, patience, and a forward-facing focus on developing a healthy church. While there might be a tendency to lean toward one group or the other, know your role is to support each group to help shape them into one.

The role of a leader is to provide vision, direction, encouragement, and guidance as both sides figure out their new role in serving in the church. Sometimes, sides will have to be brought together through strategic thinking on the leader's part, examining the strengths and weaknesses of the current needs inside the church and converts, seeing where fresh insight needs interjected. The goal is not to create factions or teams but to create a central message of serving together for the greater good of the kingdom of God.

Examining the Strengths and Weaknesses

Inside the local church, many needs will need to be met as you move towards becoming the church God has called it to be. As such, there should be an honest assessment and review of the church from the top down. The study should include all groups, leaders, classes, and activities. If the church is going to move forward, then an accurate analysis of what is happening at this moment in the church's life must be assessed. Once you have a clear idea of what is happening, the leadership team should examine the strengths and weaknesses of each leader, class, or activity and if the right person, program, or partnership is in place.

Churches that integrate visitors into members have a clear direction of where they are going. By examining the church's strengths and weaknesses, you can understand the culture better. With the new cultural understanding, the team can explore which pieces of the larger puzzle need to be positioned to meet the new season the church is entering. Sometimes, leaders will need to be rearranged into new positions, classes stopped because they are no longer meeting the immense need, and programs might need to be added to address the future focus of the church. As you examine the conditions, be open, and do not be shy because of friendships, personalities, or personal likes. Observe the church as an outside consultant so that you can provide proper direction that is not skewed by one side or the other but founded in helping the church progress forward.

Providing Fresh Insight

New attendees pick up on what is and needs to be more accurate in winning the lost to Jesus. It may take a few visits, but before long, they begin to see what the church cares about. Long-time members get transfixed in their areas and miss the broader look and feel of the overall church. Integrating the two sides into one, you start the transformation with a listening ear. The church's leadership needs to hear out all perspectives, not just those they agree with. Sure, it is uncomfortable, but with comfort comes stagnation. And stagnation breeds death. Dr. Tom Cheyney wrote, "Internal warfare has reduced many congregations to mere stagnant, status quo existence. It is crucial to understand the background of a church's battles in an effort to later describe both results and resolution."[1] Be careful not to get bogged down in the negative and miss the positive things the church is currently doing. But on the flip side, do not be afraid to tackle the issues holding the church back from future growth. When done well, this balance celebrates the past and journeys toward the future. The downside is the destruction of what could be with new people and new ideas if it's not done with an eye toward the future.

As new ideas and thought processes are brought in through new guests, and as the team provides a self-assessment review of all areas of the church, there is an excellent opportunity to see new things, add programs for the future, and subtract things that are not working. Stay open to the thoughts and words of others. To be effective long-term, you have to provide fresh leadership while maintaining the mission and vision of the local church. If you are not reading on the subject to seek other ways of doing things from your contemporaries in the field, then having a listening ear is crucial to the development of new ideas and thought processes for serving in the local church. Leadership development is continual, not just a degree earned, or a title bestowed upon a person. Degrees are only good for the time you are achieving them. Titles are only worth having if you are willing to strive to move the church forward by using them to see the broader picture.

---

1. Tom Cheyney, *Before It All Comes Crashing Down: Revitalizing a Church That Waited Too Long!* (Orlando: Renovate, 2022), 165.

The Next Best Step

Your local church has a rich history. If you were to add up all the people who have attended or been a part of your church for decades, it would number in the thousands. God used a multitude of people and gifts throughout the decades to help usher the church forward. Looking back through the years, you might see the tremendous mountaintop and low valley moments, but God provided through it all. Dr. Leslie Parrott wrote, "It is doubtful if preaching alone is going to bring the spirit of revival in any church. We need saints without halos to walk among the young, the apathetic, and the avant-garde of this generation, and demonstrate in understandable terms the transforming love of Christ."[2] Today is no different for the local church. God is sending the right people for this season that the church finds itself in. The people you have, and the people God is sending you are for this season and beyond. Focus on now. Focus on the next best step for the local church. Begin to dream again. By following God's steps today, begin to see things through fresh spiritual eyes that will help prepare for the future.

The new people the local church receives will have giftings that can fill holes, establish new ministry leads, and provide much-needed spiritual labor to help lead the church forward. Instead of fighting the unknown, the church should embrace it by meshing the current members with guests who will become members of the future. Together, the whole church will rise or fall on the ability to bring together two different groups as one.

FLOURISHING WITH A SMALL CHURCH MINDSET

So, you want the church to grow, now what? What is the next step? Where are you going now? These are straightforward questions that need answers. You have prayed as a church that God would send a person or family to the church. Guests have come. Now

---

2. Leslie Parrot, *Future Church: How Congregations Choose Their Character & Destiny* (Kansas City, MO: Beacon Hill, 1988), 102.

what? What are you supposed to do with them? To flourish again as a church, the local church and its leadership must change its mindset from growing to focusing on what it does well. Small churches grow deeper with their members and see ministry not as a buzzword but as a relationship built over time by focusing on small groups as big groups, enhancing relationships through fellowship, and championing people over programs.

Small Groups as Big Groups

The boom of the church growth mindset has created a bust of devalued properties due to a host of deferred maintenance, a decrease of members, and spiritual anorexia. Often the church still tries to be the church of two decades ago but lacks the healthy capacity to be the church of today. Instead of focusing on growing bigger, begin to focus on being better. Better in greeting newcomers. Better in sharing a meal with someone. Better at praying for the needs of the community.

How many services do you host weekly? Instead of three, try two. Or even one? Then, focus on small gatherings where members and guests can grow relationally closer to each other and God. The idea that Sunday is the only time to meet and share must be set aside for the gospel's sake. The world's schedule has changed, and adapting to the community's needs around you by revising the day or even the service location does not water down the gospel but expands the opportunity to share it with more people. As you meet at different times, try not to focus on the number of attendees but on the quality of the conversation that gains traction to dive deeper into God's word and times of group prayers. God can use your perceived smallness and allow the bigness of the calling to shine through.

Enhanced Relationships through Fellowship

People are longing for a world where they feel valued. They are valued not for what they can bring to the table but for who they are. God has placed giftings in each person that the local church needs today—many leaders and churches long for authentic relationships that make a person feel seen and heard. The small church can do that if the church members are willing to be used by the Holy Spirit to touch people more personally. Church attendance does not have to be a Sunday morning gathering. Many non-church people do not want to enter a church facility because they feel unworthy due to past choices. So, be open to finding creative ways to connect with non-church and new members. "Church members can also create offline social media groups that meet in local places of business. Sometimes people are more likely to attend meetings that are not held in church facilities, especially of they come from a non-Christian background."[3]

Stay open to meeting people where they are, not where you want them to be. Focus not on where you meet but on how you interact while you are meeting. Bond over the commonality of a sports team or children the same age. Over time, you will have an opportunity to live out your faith in such a way that the newcomer will want to know more about why you are so happy or why you seem unfrazzled when bad things happen. God has a plan, but the current members of the local church have to work God's plans and not their own. Relationships are built over time, not forced at the beginning. Trust the process and the God you serve and follow his lead. When you do, you will see that relationships through fellowship will only enhance the bond of the nonmember to the church over time.

---

3. Mark Weible, *Fishing on the Other Side: A Guide to Being the Church in the Digital Age* (Orlando: Renovate, 2019), 78.

People over Programs

Dr. Leslie Parrot wrote, "I don't believe program(s) is our problem; direction is."[4] It would help if you read that again. How many churches, maybe even yours, focus on programs as the solution to rebounding from decline? As if God values a program more than a person's soul. As a local church pastor or leader, I want you to embrace the small church mindset of valuing people over programs. To see each person and their value to the kingdom as an opportunity to live life with them by walking alongside them in the spirit of God. Let me give you permission to stop designing programs to attract new members and focus on loving the people you have, not the people you desire.

Put your energy and that of the people within the church to begin to do acts of kindness to people everywhere they go. I promise that it will make a difference to the person they are interacting with and the members doing acts of kindness over time. The fastest way to change the church is to preach the gospel without using words. As church people, let us focus not on how we feel or what we desire but to begin to serve others around us. Simple acts of kindness and small gestures can resonate with believers and unbelievers alike. This past week, a man came into the church office looking for our compassionate ministry program. The heat had gotten to him, and I felt the Spirit prompt me to ask if he would like a bottle of water—a small act but a gesture of what I want my heart to say. Less words and more actions can share with others how Christ has impacted your heart and that of the church.

See the value of being a small church leader. See the opportunities to flourish within smaller walls by serving others as Christ serves the church.

---

4. Parrot, *Future Church*, 14.

Chapter 9

Leading with Passion So Others Follow

WALKING AROUND THE CHURCH facility for the very first time, it was evident that God had blessed the church. Just over an acre of land, or nearly 50,000 square feet of space, was under a roof on the 4.26-acre property. The massive footprint from multiple buildings hid the resounding decline from the community within the church's walls. Upon becoming the pastor, it did not take long to unwind the struggles and trials of nearly three decades of steady decline. In reviewing the church's history, one cannot point to a single instance that forced the decline, but a series of missed opportunities in retrospect that caused decreases year after year. The question I had to ask myself was, "Who would want to come to a church that has declined and one that has fallen for nearly twenty-five years?" The simple answer is a church revitalizer with a heart for the medium and small church. Proverbs 29:18 (NIV) reads, "Where there is no revelation (vision), people cast off restraints; but blessed (favored) is the one who heeds wisdom's instruction." That proverb has been tattooed on the hearts and bodies of people for decades. While people do it to honor Scripture or even as a simple reminder to seek direction for the church, it is words to live by.

Bryan Rose wrote, "Imagine a day when the question 'What's your vision, pastor?' brings you energy and excitement, not dread or suspicion. Now imagine a day when every ministry understands its role in fulfilling the entire church's disciple-making call, not just its role in filling a church calendar slot."[1] The local church today needs passionate leaders who love the local church and are willing to dedicate their lives to serving the community of believers that God has given them and not the ones they wished they had. I love churches with 100 (or fewer) people. I love the close-knit relationships a pastor can build over time and the opportunity to serve the community. In a day and age where new is better, I say the church of Jesus Christ is worth serving and helping to save. But it will take vision, passion, and a commitment not to give up when things are hard. What I have learned in decades of ministry is that in the hard places, God teaches the most.

Capturing the God Vision

Inside every local church is a vision that he has for it. The question that must be asked is, will we follow it? I get it: leading is hard. But leading a person or church with no vision is next to impossible. So, lead by capturing God's vision inside the local church. Stop waiting on the people to give the vision and seek the vision that God has. Too many pastors come into a new church and force their vision on it, only to see the church revert to what it was after the pastor leaves. Think about it this way: has any member ever asked why? The simple answer is because God has been removed from the process, and carnality took over.

Vision is not dictated because someone starts or finishes an assignment. God has the right vision for each situation and season

---

1. Bryan Rose, "Overcoming Barriers to Planning Your Church's Future," *Lifeway Research*, October 23, 2023 (paras. 2–3), https://research.lifeway.com/2023/10/23/overcoming-barriers-to-planning-your-churchs-future/.

the church finds itself in, but the leadership must be willing to pray and discern God's will for the local church. Without a generous heart and spirit entuned to God, the church leadership will miss their directive from God. Be open to God's move by focusing on the main thing, obeying God, teaching the church, and serving both. When you do that, leadership transforms, and the church becomes more spiritually healthy. Be the visionary leader God has sent and not the leader you think the church needs.

Capturing the Passion of Opportunity

The catalyst of a revitalization turnaround is excitement. It seems rather elementary, but it's revolutionary as the palpable excitement overtakes the doom and gloom of what was for what is to come. Inside the broader group of the church is the leadership vision that will take the church to the next level, but it must be harnessed, encouraged to grow, and shared from the pulpit to the pew. God has an incredible plan for the local church, even those struggling to stay open. Trust me, when the pastor becomes on fire for the future, the people can't help but get caught up in the wildfire of optimism.

Optimism and action create a one-two punch of forward opportunity that pushes back the negative voices and dark forces that have kept the church from moving ahead. I have seen passion and opportunity transform the church in my current revitalization assignment, which has moved the church forward with new plans that others have said, "We talked about it but could never seem to move forward." What changed? The plans stayed the same, but the passion for which the plans were talked about and implemented captured a new opportunity cycle that has delivered results. God has the plan inside your local church, but as a leader, you must claim the mantle of leadership and lead with passion and opportunity to move the church forward on small and large projects. The days of playing it safe are gone, and the God- days are ahead.

Capturing the Commitment to Serve

If you are leading a local church or ministry, you must decide if it is worth saving. I am not asking for your opinion but for God's direction. There is a tendency to close a church down rather than to invest in revitalizing the church. I have heard it said that it is easier to plant a healthy church than recreate it in a dying church. Instead of throwing the proverbial baby out with the bath water, why not begin to pray like never before for God's guidance to love the people and community you have while preparing for future guests? What do you or the church have to lose?

Think about it this way: people inside and outside your local church need a Bible-believing church serving as the hands and feet of Jesus. The community needs a church that captures the community's needs and strives to meet a portion of the needs through praying, giving, and sowing of their time through volunteerism. If the pastor is not leading by example, how do you expect the people to maintain consistency once the excitement of trying something new wears off? The leader must share the vision and live it out for the people to capture it within their DNA. Vision once cast is only fulfilled when it is lived out through the leader's example. Challenge yourself to be a leader who leads in prayer, serving, and repeating the cycle so that others may follow.

LEADING WITH AN EYE TOWARD THE GOAL OF WINNING AND KEEPING GUESTS

Leading any organization is challenging, but leading a church where the workers are majority volunteers can create the desire for change in a leader. Yet, change can only come once the leader understands that what they do and how they do it are as important as achieving the goal. As a leader, you might be driven by the goal of preparing and winning guests, but do not allow the dream or desire to override relationships or relational experiences for those who interact with you over time.

Capture the Moment by Staying Present in the Pursuit

As a leader, I have had more seasons than I care to count, that allowed my dreams to get in the way of my current reality. I have seen the disappointment in my wife when I did not make it home in time for dinner or missed a recital practice because I allowed "more important things" to get in the way of my family. Learning the hard way, I realized that my priorities were out of balance and that what seemed necessary today may not stand the test of time. Do not read into what is not being said, but the time of a leader is more valuable than a leader gives credit.

What is God's dream inside of you? It might start as winning guests, but maybe it turns to keeping them. Or something "big" that needs to be accomplished in the church's life. Chasing a goal and accomplishing a dream is never more critical than finding balance in managing your time and pursuits. Stay present while playing with your children or talking to a church member. Do not allow your mind to wander into conversations or a to-do list while focusing on the essential thing right before you. Countless leaders have failed not because they did too much but because they needed to focus on the small thing before them. It was the small act that led to a big failure. I pray you keep moving toward your dream but do it in a way that honors your time with others.

Complete the Task and Move Closer to the Goal

There is a saying that you can look inside anyone's car or office and tell what type of leader they are. Why? Because the disorganized leader lives a life that fails to prioritize the most crucial task, while the organized leader has a clear structure. Regardless of how many tasks are parked on your to-do list right now, you need to realize you cannot accomplish every job simultaneously and still maintain the quality expected of your work.

Prioritizing your to-do list enables you to move up and down the list of the most essential tasks in your current season.

Currently, I am leading my church through a significant revitalization rework. Viewing our situation, I realized they needed more time to prepare for everything, but they were ready for something.

I took over twenty-five tasks that needed to be completed, divided them into three major phases, and then prioritized that list from greatest need to least. Each significant task in each phase is important, but not all have the same value at each stage. To move closer to the goal, you must find balance, complete the task before you, observe the issue, and begin working towards that goal. If you want guests and to keep them, then do not skip this stage because you think you have it all together. Slow down, focus, plan, and then execute that plan.

Compare Where You Are to Where You Want to Be Over Time

I wish you could magically snap your fingers and things would change so much that people would just pour in through the church doors. However, without working the plan, the plan is just a plan. As you progress toward your goals, spend time quarterly or more frequently self-evaluating where you currently are and where you want to be over time. In this self-evaluation period, observe what brings you joy daily and write those things down. What part of your routine brings you stress or even laziness? Write those down. Then observe what is related to the goal. If you need to change the task or the goal, you can change the mission or the purpose. Far too many leaders stay focused on the wrong thing because it was their dream a decade ago, but today they find themselves in a different season of life.

Over the last several years, I had the honor of writing five books, teaching and training on church revitalization, and launching a podcast directly related to what I love. Several colleagues have asked, how? The simple answer is I set a ten-year goal with benchmarks and have slowly worked toward my ten-year goal. Sure, there have been times when there was no progress and others when everyone saw it. Consistency has been my driving force.

Consistency has enabled me to evaluate where I am at to where I want to go, and I keep moving forward.

As a leader, make it a practice to hone in on your calling and focus on everything you do to accomplish that goal. Spend time evaluating and reacting to what you find and adjusting yourself to stay on track.

Celebrate the Things You've Accomplished

As a leader, you might only be satisfied once you complete the entire journey toward your dream, but still pause and celebrate what you have accomplished as you go along. Use the acronym **P.A.U.S.E.** to help you remember to celebrate.

Praise what God has done and will do in the future. Too many leaders forget how far they have come and miss out on what God is doing even now. Step into your new season by looking back to celebrate your accomplishments and look up to the one who provided them. Praise the fact that five guests have come and three have been retained. As you praise, say to God and the members that something good is happening.

Act to draw attention toward God, others, and what they have done to help move the ministry forward. Be a leader who celebrates others before yourself while acknowledging God and using others to help you as a leader. Remember you cannot build the church alone. But, with a passionate group of people acting on the will of God, things begin to transform one person or guests at a time.

Understand that moving an organization or dream forward takes time, but stay on task doing your part. Do not succumb to the temptation of rushing, but slow down, do your part, and allow God to move. The hardest portion of the P.A.U.S.E. acronym is to understand that God moves in his timing not yours. You might be doing everything right, but if God is not ready nothing will be accomplished that will be sustained. Trust the God- process. Be ready to move when God is ready to act. When you do your part, and he is doing his, nothing can stop the forward momentum that is developed.

Savor what you have accomplished before you move on to the next thing. Many leaders miss the mark because they have not marked down what they have accomplished and then fail to recognize the move of God before chasing after the next thing. Winning one guest is a big deal. Sure, you may want exponential growth, but any growth is praiseworthy. As you complete even the smallest project, savor the moment. Allow others to see what God has done. Do not rush on to the next thing, because you will miss an important step in building momentum for that next project.

Excel in what God has called you to do. Focus on the God-task and march forward to complete the job. Celebrate milestones along the way while you focus on accomplishing the goal. Not every church or leader can be everything to everyone in the community, but be the someone that one guest will need. Excel not on trying to be someone else or some church that will attract a certain part of the population, but be the answer the community needs. Excel at what you do well and allow other ministries to do what they do well. Remember the local church is not competing against itself, but in winning the lost of the community.

HOW FAST SHOULD YOU CHANGE THINGS IN CHURCH?

Every visionary pastor has had to contend with how fast change should be enacted within the church. Some pastors change everything so quickly that they are out before they unpack their office boxes. Still, others take so long to encourage changing anything they become part of the institution that has pushed back on change in the first place. So, how fast should a pastor promote change in the church as they turn their eagerness to future guests? Dr. Thom Rainer, an expert in church revitalization, would say it "depends." It depends on many factors that only the revitalizer will know as they are inside serving the local church. Revitalization strategists can offer timeframe suggestions, but only the revitalizer, through the guidance of the Holy Spirit, can determine the right time to move forward. However, there are three things to consider as a revitalizer moves forward.

Steady Change Is Change

There is a tendency to try to rush change within the church. The revitalizer sees the need and is called to help lead the church through change but may not fully understand the history behind a piece of furniture or why things are done in a particular way. Only through conversations can questions be asked and listening take place that a broader picture emerges. Instead of fretting over the pace of change, begin to see a steady progression forward as a positive, and not negative, movement of God. Progress is not regression and should be celebrated as steps in the right direction.

While change is propagated in church members' lives daily, the inside of the church stays stagnant for the most part. People sit in the same pew, classrooms are never updated, and programs are often repeated, even if a small handful of people are participating. Long-term members might even resist the slightest deviation from regular activities and thus drive the revitalization pastor out of the church because there are too many changes or even too many new people attending, even though they hired the pastor to be a change agent. Instead of becoming a statistic, become a steady change agent that embraces the uniqueness of the local church and culture. See change not as one-and-done but a long-term movement forward to achieve the goals that the local church has for themselves. Steady change is strategic, and spirit-led. Through a willing heart, a visionary spirit, and obedience to God, the church and pastor can lead change that helps the church reach its community like never before.

Strategic Action Steps

There is no actual timetable for "fixing" things inside the local church or when a guest will decide to stay after visiting the church. You must remember that the church's decline did not happen overnight and will not be reversed in the first quarter of your leadership or even the first year. But progress will be made over time through proper planning, visionary leadership, and obedience of God's people. I use a 3P process that you might find helpful in your revitalization efforts.

- Plan—Develop an action plan of all activities that need to be accomplished in the next five years. Realize that things will move up and down the list depending on needs, and items may need to be added because they were unforeseen. Put the plan into action by taking concrete steps to accomplish the low-hanging fruit, which will help develop trust with the members and excitement for future accomplishments. Put the effort in to win people and win progress. Let me remind you again, with any plan without action, it's just a plan.

- Produce—Without action; results will not ever come about. Make sure you produce early wins. Wins create a sense of momentum that encourages the discouraged, provides hope for the future, and excites the ones who brought you in to be the change agent.

- Progress—Each step taken is a step into the future. Be strategic in taking actions that honor the past, celebrate the present, and lean into the future. Create an atmosphere of honoring the church's history and those who have stayed during the decline. Enable them to feel part of the growth that will come by having them submit ideas or be a part of preparing for guests as the church gears up to connect with the community.

Stimulate Cooperation and Community

As the decline happened in the church, blame became the consistent message that was heard repeatedly. Blaming the community for changing, blaming members for leaving, and blaming the denomination for not helping. Instead of blaming others, allow the church to pray, repenting of past wrongs and praying that God would help them submit and commit to the changes to come. The most significant role of a revitalizing pastor is to preach, teach, share, and commit to unity in the body. It is not always easy, but through a godly example, people will see faithfulness in action. A note of caution: unity at all costs is too costly to the revitalization effort, but unity in the mission, vision, and godly direction is essential as you remake the church to welcome new people.

The heart behind any revitalization effort is to see the church reach the community and new people with the gospel. It should not be about membership, tithing, or even more people in the pews. Those will come if the church is willing to prepare for guests for the greater good of the community. Let me say this: there is no magic formula in winning and keeping new guests, but I pray you have found strategies in this resource that have made you think about what more you could do to prepare, retain, and invite guests into the local church.

Epilogue

As you begin to dream about future guests and preparing for them to arrive, it is an opportunity to pause and refocus on your ministry and direction of the church through prayer, obeying God, and dreaming dreams of what is to come. Let me give you three quick and easy ways to focus your ministry as you prepare to focus on future guests.

Focus on What Works Locally

Do not allow someone else's success to dictate your definition of success. How often have you looked at a church's social media page from down the street, seen the "amazing" things happening on their campus, and asked, "Why not here, God?" Or what about when you read another pastor's social media post and instantly get envious of their "success"? Know this truth: God has not forgotten about you or your local church. He has called you for a time like this to lead your local church back from the abyss of decline into a period of reawakening.

Realize that what may work at one church, even in the same town, may not work in your current assignment. Focus on what works locally, but be willing to assess the needs of your local community (church family, and neighborhood) and help connect them with the broader community. Lead your church to specialize in an area as you prepare to win guests. Sure, you may want a multigenerational church, but if you do not have it today, lean into what you have and can do best. The church might not have a lot of children, but it has a lot of senior members. Why not become the best senior church it can be? Begin reviewing the physical foundation of the church, and evaluate the infrastructure. Maybe you could take out steps and replace them with ramps so it is easier for guests and members to get in and out of the church. Host hymn sings, take day trips that are open to the community that seniors would want to attend, develop small groups geared to the desires of that age group, add large font to bulletins and signage, etc.

Churches get caught up trying to catch the younger group and miss a large swath of the population that needs a substantial church home. If you have a younger age demographic in your local church, you might lean the other way with new playground equipment, incredible children's wings and classrooms, and creative outreach activities geared towards the younger set. Either way, find out what is working and focus on that. Think about the future and act with future guests in mind.

Focus on Who You Are Trying to Reach

The preparation season is as important as the promised season you hope to lead the church into. Preparation is foundational work that strategically positions the church for future advancement and creative opportunities that will impact the community and ministries of the church. As you narrow your focus and move from this encouraging resource and put into action who you can reach today, begin to lay the groundwork for a future shift that will help the church move toward a more multigenerational model. That may mean saving funds for a future remodeling of currently underutilized areas—setting aside funds for a forthcoming children's pastor or senior adult pastor, depending on what side of the generational gap your church is on, and beginning to dream dreams again of what the church could be in the future.

Many churches get into trouble because they lean too far to one side of the generational gap and are unable or sometimes

Epilogue

unwilling to progress toward the middle to find balance when preparing for guests. Use the concepts in this resource to rethink strategies that will lay the foundation for a future realigning of the church. Do not rush this process, and make sure you include multiple layers of staff, board members, and lay church members in the dreaming process. Evaluate the community demographics, neighborhood needs, future desires and vision of the church when you are thinking through the following steps. Keep an eye on what could happen twelve to twenty-four months from now. Plan what resources must be brought forth, setting aside funds, space, and other resources to move the idea into action and be prepared for what God will do with the church's faithfulness. God is bringing you people, so get ready for them now. Do not wait until they arrive.

Focus on the Core Values of the Church

Who the church is today is as important as who it will be tomorrow. Knowing God's call on the church, the community it was birthed into, and the reality of the ever-shifting landscape within a community's social, economic, and spiritual fabric is a crucial component to living out the core values found in the statements of belief of the church. The church's values are as important as its mission and vision statement. The statements provide direction, but only the values lived from them clarify the call God is leading the church. As change happens in and out of the church, there could be a tendency to retreat from the value set found in God's word. Do not shrink back from the church's biblical mandate to lead others to Christ by preaching the gospel, seeking God's forgiveness of sin, and allowing the work of the Holy Spirit to work in the lives of those in and out of the church.

God has an incredible plan for the local church. As the world moves closer and closer to a post-Christian world, the local church will have to adhere to its core values to stay true to God's word and the calling placed on the church's mandate from God. As you help the church walk through these days, help to reinvest in the values found in Scripture by praying, seeking God's will, working together, and investing in others outside the church's walls.

This next season your local church is moving into can be an incredibly fruitful part of your ministry if you help the church refocus now to believe again tomorrow, and to prepare for the guests who are coming.

About the Author

DR. DESMOND BARRETT is the lead pastor at Winter Haven Nazarene in Winter Haven, Florida. He is a podcast host of *Revitalizing the Declining Church with Dr. Desmond Barrett*, has done extensive research in the area of church revitalization, and serves as church revitalizer, consultant, coach, and mentor to revitalizing pastors and churches.

He is a graduate of Nazarene Bible College (bachelor of ministry) and Trevecca Nazarene University (master of organizational leadership, and EdD in leadership and professional practice).

Other Books by the Author

Confidence for Leadership: Influencing with Skill and Integrity (coauthor)

Missional Reset: Capturing the Heart for Local Missions in the Established Church (coauthor)

Revitalize to Plant: Reshaping the Established Church to Plant Churches (coauthor)

Addition through Subtraction: Revitalizing the Established Church

Revitalizing the Declining Church: From Death's Door to Community Growth

www.ingramcontent.com/pod-product-compliance
Lightning Source LLC
Chambersburg PA
CBHW071731090426
42738CB00011B/2451